PUNISHING
PRESSURE POINTS

PRACTICAL PAIN COMPLIANCE
PRESSURE POINT TECHNIQUES
SAMMY FRANCO

Also by Sammy Franco

Engage With Rage
War Machine II
1001 Street Fighting Secrets
Combat Pressure Points
Cane Fighting
Double End Bag Training
The Heavy Bag Bible
The Widow Maker Compendium
Invincible: Mental Toughness Techniques for Peak Performance
Unleash Hell: A Step-by-Step Guide to Devastating Widow Maker Combinations
Feral Fighting: Advanced Widow Maker Fighting Techniques
The Widow Maker Program: Extreme Self-Defense for Deadly Force Situations
Savage Street Fighting: Tactical Savagery as a Last Resort
Heavy Bag Combinations
Heavy Bag Training
The Complete Body Opponent Bag Book
Stand and Deliver: A Street Warrior's Guide to Tactical Combat Stances
Maximum Damage: Hidden Secrets Behind Brutal Fighting Combinations
First Strike: End a Fight in Ten Seconds or Less
The Bigger They Are, The Harder They Fall
Self-Defense Tips and Tricks
Kubotan Power: Quick & Simple Steps to Mastering the Kubotan Keychain
Gun Safety: For Home Defense and Concealed Carry
Out of the Cage: A Guide to Beating a Mixed Martial Artist on the Street
Warrior Wisdom: Inspiring Ideas from the World's Greatest Warriors
War Machine: How to Transform Yourself Into a Vicious Street Fighter
When Seconds Count: Self-Defense for the Real World
Killer Instinct: Unarmed Combat for Street Survival
Street Lethal: Unarmed Urban Combat

Punishing Pressure Points
Copyright © 2024 by Sammy Franco
ISBN: 978-1-941845-87-5
Printed in the United States of America
Visit online at: ContemporaryFightingArts.com

For The Constant Reader.
Thank you!

PUNISHING PRESSURE POINTS

Contents

"The more technique you have, the less you have to worry about it."

– Pablo Picasso

Disclaimer

The author, publisher, and distributors of this book will accept no responsibility, nor are they liable to any person or entity whatsoever for any injury, damage, or loss of any sort that may arise out of practicing, teaching, or disseminating of any techniques or ideas contained herein.

You assume full responsibility for the use of the information in this book and agree that the author, distributor and contributors hold no liability to you for claims, damages, costs and expenses, legal fees, or any other costs incurred due to or in any way related to your reliance on anything derived from this book or its contents.

Additionally, it is the reader's responsibility to research and comply with all local, state, and federal laws and regulations pertaining to the use of self-defense techniques. This book is for educational reference information only!

Before you begin any exercise or activity, including those suggested in this book, it is important to check with your physician to see if you have any condition that might be aggravated by strenuous training. The information contained in this book is not designed to diagnose, treat, or manage any physical health conditions.

About This Book

Welcome back to my Pressure Points Fighting system. I assume that by now you have read my first book in the series titled, *Combat Pressure Points*. If not, I encourage you to do so before launching forward with this advanced book.

Punishing Pressure Points teaches you my unique and effective pain compliance pressure point system specifically designed for "real world" street self-defense. The skills and techniques featured in this book are simple and can be readily used by anyone, regardless of size or strength and level of experience. Most importantly, you don't need martial arts training to apply many of these effective pressure point techniques.

Unlike other pressure point books, *Punishing Pressure Points* is devoid of impractical and gimmicky techniques that can get you injured or possibly killed when faced with a real-world self-defense crisis. Instead, this book arms you with the most efficient, effective, and practical pressure point techniques that work in the chaos of a real-world survival situation. In fact, the self-defense skills and techniques found within these pages are straightforward and easy to apply.

Punishing Pressure Points is predicated on my 30+ years of research, training and teaching reality-based self-defense and combat sciences. In fact, I've taught these unique pressure point techniques to thousands of my students, and I'm confident they can help you and your loved ones during an emergency situation.

Regularly practicing the pressure point skills featured in this book will establish a rock solid foundation for using them in self-defense. Moreover, the techniques featured in this book will significantly improve your overall personal protection skills, enhance your conditioning, and introduce you to an exciting

PUNISHING PRESSURE POINTS

method of self-defense.

This book is also a skill-building workbook. So feel free to write in the margins, underline passages, and dog-ear the pages. I strongly recommend that you read this text from beginning to end, chapter by chapter. Only after you have read the entire book, should you treat it like a reference and skip around, reading those sections that interest you.

Finally, the information, techniques, and suggestions contained herein are dangerous and should only be used to protect yourself or a loved one from the immediate risk of unlawful injury. Remember, the decision to use physical force for self-defense must always be a last resort, after all other means of avoiding violence have been exhausted.

Walk in peace!

Sammy Franco
ContemporaryFightingArts.com

INTRODUCTION

What is
Contemporary Fighting Arts?

Exploring Contemporary Fighting Arts

Before diving head first into this book, I'd like to first introduce you to my unique system of fighting, Contemporary Fighting Arts (CFA). I hope it will give you a greater understanding and appreciation of the material covered in this book. And for those of you who are already familiar with my CFA system, you can skip to chapter one.

Contemporary Fighting Arts® (CFA), is a state-of-the-art combat system that was introduced to the world in 1983. This sophisticated and practical system of self-defense is designed specifically to provide efficient and effective methods to avoid, defuse, confront, and neutralize both armed and unarmed assailants in a variety of deadly situations and circumstances.

Unlike karate, kung-fu, mixed martial arts and the like, CFA is the first offensive-based American martial art that is specifically designed for the violence that plagues our cruel city streets. CFA dispenses with the extraneous and the impractical and focuses on real-life street fighting.

Every technique and tactic found within the CFA system must meet three essential criteria for fighting: efficiency, effectiveness, and safety. Efficiency means that the techniques permit you to reach your combative objective quickly and economically. Effectiveness means that the elements of the system will produce the desired effect. Finally, Safety means that the combative elements provide the least amount of danger and risk for you - the fighter.

CFA is not about tournaments or senseless competition. It doesn't require you to waste time and energy practicing forms (katas) or other impractical rituals. There are no theatrical kicks or exotic techniques. Finally, CFA doesn't adhere blindly to tradition for tradition's sake. Simply put, it's a scientific yet pragmatic approach to staying alive on the streets.

CFA has been taught to people of all walks of life. Some include the U.S. Border Patrol, police officers, deputy sheriffs, security guards, military personnel, private investigators, surgeons, lawyers, college professors, airline pilots, as well as black belts, boxers, and kick boxers. CFA's broad appeal results from its ability to teach people how to really fight.

It's All In The Name

Before discussing the three components that make up Contemporary Fighting Arts, it is important to understand how CFA acquired its unique name. To begin, the first word, "Contemporary," was selected because it refers to the system's modern, up-to-date orientation. Unlike traditional martial arts, CFA is specifically designed to meet the challenges of our modern world.

The second term, "Fighting," was chosen because it accurately describes the system's combat orientation. After all, why not just call it Contemporary Martial Arts? There are two reasons for this. First, the word "martial" conjures up images of traditional and impractical martial art forms that are antithetical to the system. Second, why dilute a perfectly functional name when the word "fighting" defines the system so succinctly? Contemporary Fighting Arts is about teaching people how to really fight.

Let's look at the last word, "Arts." In the subjective sense, "art" refers to the combat skills that are acquired through arduous study, practice, and observation. The bottom line is that effective street fighting skills will require consistent practice and attention. Take, for example, something as seemingly basic as an elbow strike, which will actually require hundreds of hours of practice to perfect.

The pluralization of the word "Art" reflects CFA's protean instruction. The various components of CFA's training (i.e., firearms training, stick fighting, ground fighting, natural body weapon mastery, and so on) have all truly earned their status as individual art forms and, as such, require years of consistent study and practice to perfect. To acquire a greater understanding of CFA, here is an overview of the system's three vital components: the physical, the mental, and the spiritual.

The Physical Component

The physical component of CFA focuses on the physical development of a fighter, including physical fitness, weapon and technique mastery, and self-defense attributes.

Physical Fitness

If you are going to prevail in a street fight, you must be physically fit. It's that simple. In fact, you will never master the tools and skills of combat unless you're in excellent physical shape. On the average, you will have to spend more than an hour a day to achieve maximum fitness.

In CFA physical fitness comprises the following three broad

components: cardiorespiratory conditioning, muscular/skeletal conditioning, and proper body composition.

The cardiorespiratory system includes the heart, lungs, and circulatory system, which undergo tremendous stress during the course of a street fight. So you're going to have to run, jog, bike, swim, or skip rope to develop sound cardiorespiratory conditioning. Each aerobic workout should last a minimum of 30 minutes and be performed at least four times per week.

The second component of physical fitness is muscular/skeletal conditioning. In the streets, the strong survive and the rest go to the morgue. To strengthen your bones and muscles to withstand the rigors of a real fight, your program must include progressive resistance (weight training) and calisthenics. You will also need a stretching program designed to loosen up every muscle group. You can't kick, punch, ground fight, or otherwise execute the necessary body mechanics if you're "tight" or inflexible. Stretching on a regular basis will also increase the muscles' range of motion, improve circulation, reduce the possibility of injury, and relieve daily stress.

The final component of physical fitness is proper body composition: simply, the ratio of fat to lean body tissue. Your diet and training regimen will affect your level or percentage of body fat significantly. A sensible and consistent exercise program accompanied by a healthy and balanced diet will facilitate proper body composition. Do not neglect this important aspect of physical fitness.

Weapon and Technique Mastery

You won't stand a chance against a vicious assailant if you don't master the techniques of fighting. In CFA, we teach our students both armed and unarmed methods of combat. Unarmed fighting requires that you master a complete arsenal of natural body weapons and techniques. In conjunction, you must also learn the various stances, hand positioning, footwork, body mechanics, defensive structure, locks, chokes, and various holds. Keep in mind that something as simple as a basic punch will actually require hundreds of hours to perfect.

Range proficiency is another important aspect of weapon and technique mastery. Briefly, range proficiency is the ability to fight effectively in all three ranges of unarmed fighting. Although punching range tools are emphasized in CFA, kicking and grappling ranges cannot be neglected. Our kicking range tools consist of deceptive and powerful low-line kicks. Grappling range tools include head-butts, elbows, knees, foot stomps, biting, tearing, gouging, and crushing tactics.

Although CFA focuses on striking, we also teach our students a myriad of chokes, locks, and holds that can be used in a ground fight. While such grappling range submission techniques are not the most preferred methods of dealing with a ground fighting situation, they must be developed.

Defensive tools and skills are also taught. Our defensive structure is efficient, uncomplicated, and impenetrable. It provides the fighter maximum protection while allowing complete freedom of choice for acquiring offensive control. Our defensive structure is based on distance, parrying, blocking, evading, mobility, and stance structure. Simplicity is always the key.

Students are also instructed in specific methods of armed fighting. For example, CFA provides instruction about firearms for personal and household protection. We provide specific guidelines for handgun purchasing, operation, nomenclature, proper caliber, shooting fundamentals, cleaning, and safe storage. Our firearm program also focuses on owner responsibility and the legal ramifications regarding the use of deadly force.

CFA's weapons program also consists of natural body weapons, knives and edged weapons, single and double stick, makeshift weaponry, the side-handle baton, and oleoresin capsicum (OC) spray.

Combat Attributes

Your offensive and defensive tools are useless unless they are used strategically. For any tool or technique to be effective in a real fight, it must be accompanied by specific attributes. Attributes are qualities that enhance a particular tool, technique, or maneuver. Some examples include speed, power, timing, coordination, accuracy, non-telegraphic movement, balance, and target orientation.

CFA also has a wide variety of training drills and methodologies designed to develop and sharpen these combat attributes. For example, our students learn to ground fight while blindfolded, spar with one arm tied down, and fight while handcuffed.

Reality is the key. For example, in class students participate in full-contact drills against fully padded assailants, and real weapon disarms are rehearsed and analyzed in a variety of dangerous scenarios. Students also train with a large variety of equipment, including heavy bags, double-end bags, uppercut bags, pummel bags, focus mitts, striking shields, mirrors, rattan sticks, training bats, kicking pads, knife drones, trigger-sensitive (mock) guns, full-body armor, and numerous environmental props.

There are more than two hundred unique training methodologies used in Contemporary Fighting Arts. Each one is scientifically designed to prepare students for the hard-core realities of real world combat. There are also three specific training methodologies used to develop and sharpen the fundamental attributes and skills of armed and unarmed fighting, including proficiency training, conditioning training, and street training.

Proficiency training can be used for both armed and unarmed skills. When conducted properly, proficiency training develops speed, power, accuracy, non-telegraphic movement, balance, and general psychomotor skill. The training objective is to sharpen one specific body weapon, maneuver, or technique at a time by executing it over and over for a prescribed number of repetitions. Each time the technique or maneuver is executed with "clean" form at various speeds. Movements are also performed with the eyes closed to develop a kinesthetic "feel" for the action. Proficiency training can be accomplished through the use of various types of equipment, including the heavy bag, double-end bag, focus mitts, training knives, real and mock pistols, striking shields, shin and knee guards, foam and plastic bats, mannequin heads, and so on.

Conditioning training develops endurance, fluidity, rhythm, distancing, timing, speed, footwork, and balance. In most cases, this type of training requires the student to deliver a variety of fighting combinations for three- or four-minute rounds separated by 30-second breaks. Like proficiency training, this type of training can also be performed at various speeds. A good workout consists of at least five rounds. Conditioning training can be performed on the bags with full-contact sparring gear, rubber training knives, focus mitts, kicking shields, and shin guards, or against imaginary assailants in shadow fighting.

Conditioning training is not necessarily limited to just three-

9

or four-minute rounds. For example, CFA's ground fighting training can last as long as 30 minutes. The bottom line is that it all depends on what you are training for.

Street training is the final preparation for the real thing. Since many violent altercations are explosive, lasting an average of 20 seconds, you must prepare for this possible scenario. This means delivering explosive and powerful compound attacks with vicious intent for approximately 20 seconds, resting one minute, and then repeating the process.

Street training prepares you for the stress and immediate fatigue of a real fight. It also develops speed, power, explosiveness, target selection and recognition, timing, footwork, pacing, and breath control. You should practice this methodology in different lighting, on different terrains, and in different environmental settings. You can use different types of training equipment as well. For example, you can prepare yourself for multiple assailants by having your training partners attack you with focus mitts from a variety of angles, ranges, and target postures. For 20 seconds, go after them with low-line kicks, powerful punches, and devastating strikes.

When all is said and done, the physical component creates a fighter who is physically fit and armed with an arsenal of techniques that can be deployed with destructive results.

The Mental Component

The mental component of CFA focuses on the cerebral aspects of a fighter, developing killer instinct, strategic/tactical awareness, analysis and integration skills, philosophy, and cognitive skills.

The Killer Instinct

Deep within each of us is a cold and deadly primal power known as the "killer instinct." The killer instinct is a vicious combat mentality that surges to your consciousness and turns you into a fierce fighter who is free of fear, anger, and apprehension. If you want to survive the horrifying dynamics of real criminal violence, you must cultivate and utilize this instinctive killer mentality.

Visualization and crisis rehearsal are just two techniques used to develop, refine, and channel this extraordinary source of strength and energy so that it can be used to its full potential.

Strategic/Tactical Awareness

Strategy is the bedrock of preparedness. In CFA, there are three unique categories of strategic awareness that will diminish the likelihood of criminal victimization. They are criminal awareness, situational awareness, and self-awareness. When developed, these essential skills prepare you to assess a wide variety of threats instantaneously and accurately. Once you've made a proper threat assessment, you will be able to choose one of the following five self-defense options: comply, escape, de-escalate, assert, or fight back.

CFA also teaches students to assess a variety of other important factors, including the assailant's demeanor, intent, range, positioning and weapon capability, as well as such environmental issues as escape routes, barriers, terrain, and makeshift weaponry. In addition to assessment skills, CFA also teaches students how to enhance perception and observation skills.

Analysis and Integration Skills

The analytical process is intricately linked to understanding how to defend yourself in any threatening situation. If you want to be the best, every aspect of fighting and personal protection must be dissected. Every strategy, tactic, movement, and concept must be broken down to its atomic parts. The three planes (physical, mental, spiritual) of self-defense must be unified scientifically through arduous practice and constant exploration.

CFA's most advanced practitioners have sound insight and understanding of a wide range of sciences and disciplines. They include human anatomy, kinesiology, criminal justice, sociology, kinesics, proxemics, combat physics, emergency medicine, crisis management, histrionics, police and military science, the psychology of aggression, and the role of archetypes.

Analytical exercises are also a regular part of CFA training. For example, we conduct problem-solving sessions involving particular assailants attacking in defined environments. We move hypothetical attackers through various ranges to provide insight into tactical solutions. We scrutinize different methods of attack for their general utility in combat. We also discuss the legal ramifications of self-defense on a frequent basis.

In addition to problem-solving sessions, students are slowly exposed to concepts of integration and modification. Oral and written examinations are given to measure intellectual accomplishment. Unlike systems, CFA does not use colored belts or sashes to identify the student's level of proficiency.

Philosophy

Philosophical resolution is essential to a fighter's mental confidence and clarity. Anyone learning the art of war must find the ultimate answers to questions concerning the use of violence in defense of himself or others. To advance to the highest levels of combat awareness, you must find clear and lucid answers to such provocative questions as could you take the life of another, what are your fears, who are you, why are you interested in studying Contemporary Fighting Arts, why are you reading this book, and what is good and what is evil? If you haven't begun the quest to formulate these important questions and answers, then take a break. It's time to figure out just why you want to know the laws and rules of destruction.

Cognitive Combat Skills

Cognitive combat exercises are also important for improving one's fighting skills. CFA uses visualization and crisis rehearsal scenarios to improve general body mechanics, tools and techniques, and maneuvers, as well as tactic selection. Mental clarity, concentration, and emotional control are also developed to enhance one's ability to call upon the controlled killer instinct.

The Spiritual Component

There are many tough fighters out there. In fact, they reside in every town in every country. However, most are nothing more than vicious animals that lack self-mastery. And self-mastery is what separates the true warrior from the eternal novice.

I am not referring to religious precepts or beliefs when I speak of CFA's spiritual component. Unlike most martial arts, CFA does not merge religion into its spiritual aspect. Religion is a very personal and private matter and should never, be incorporated into any fighting system. CFA's spiritual component is not something that is taught or studied. Rather, it is that which transcends the physical and mental aspects of being and reality. There is a deeper part of each of us that is a tremendous source of truth and accomplishment.

In CFA, the spiritual component is something that is slowly and progressively acquired. During the challenging quest of combat training, one begins to tap the higher qualities of human nature. Those elements of our being that inherently enable us to know right from wrong and good from evil. As we slowly develop this aspect of our total self, we begin to strengthen qualities profoundly important to the "truth." Such qualities are essential to your growth through the mastery of inner peace, the clarity of your "vision," and your recognition of universal truths.

One of the goals of my system is to promote virtue and moral responsibility in people who have extreme capacities for physical and mental destructiveness. The spiritual component of fighting is truly the most difficult aspect of personal growth. Yet, unlike the physical component, where the practitioner's abilities will be limited to some degree by genetics and other natural factors, the spiritual component of combat offers unlimited potential for growth and development.

In the final analysis, CFA's spiritual component poses the greatest challenges for the student. It is an open-ended plane of unlimited advancement.

CHAPTER ONE
Pain Compliance Pressure Points

UNDERSTANDING PRESSURE POINTS

Having a solid understanding of pressure point fighting techniques is important for anyone interested in real-world self-defense. In my previous book, *Combat Pressure Points* I gave the reader a very detailed breakdown of my pressure point fighting system, and some of it bears repeating.

What are Pressure Points?

Pressure points have long been shrouded in mystery, misunderstanding, and a boatload of bullshit. Therefore, I'm going to save you a lot of time and cut to the chase with a simple, clear-cut definition that can be easily understood.

For all intents and purposes, a "pressure point" is a vulnerable anatomical target, such as nerve cluster, joint or any other sensitive tissue target that can be struck, compressed, or wrenched with force during a self-defense situation.

For example, the throat is considered a compression pressure point that can be exploited with a rear naked choke hold, requiring you to simultaneously compress both the carotid artery and vegus nerve with both your forearms.

Moreover, a strong and prolonged compression to a pressure point target may cause some of the following physiological responses to occur:

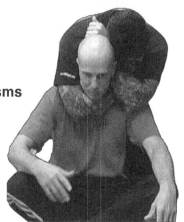

- **Motor dysfunction**
- **Balance disruption**
- **Extreme pain**
- **Involuntary muscular spasms**
- **Drooling**
- **Disorientation**
- **Loss of consciousness**
- **Loss of bodily functions**
- **Possible death**

Two Pressure Point Categories

Now that you have an understanding that pressure points can be either struck, compressed or wrenched, it's time to look into the two possible categories, each with different self-defense objectives. They include:

- **Incapacitation Pressure Points**
- **Pain Compliance Pressure Points**

Incapacitation Pressure Points

Incapacitation pressure points is a ubiquitous term and will mean different things to different people. For example,

18

according to some practitioners, incapacitation pressure points are targets which cause brief dizziness for the adversary; a dizziness that causes the opponent's knees to weaken or buckle.

Sadly, such a definition is inaccurate and certainly impractical for real world self-defense applications. Pressure point fighting techniques that simply promote "transitory dizziness" are inadequate for real-world self-defense conditions. Never forget this.

In most cases, transitory dizziness won't work on psychotics, drunks or drugged assailants as well as many other real world scenarios. For example, consider the dangers of applying one of those "dizzying techniques" on an enraged attacker high on PCP. Frankly, you'll have a snowball's chance in hell of surviving the encounter.

In real world self-defense, time is a critical factor! You must employ practical street fighting techniques that produce instant results. Therefore, the only safe and sure-fire method of incapacitation pressure point fighting are those techniques that produce immediate results... 100% Incapacitation!

And since we're only concerned with real world self-defense applications, I define *incapacitation pressure points* as anatomical targets which cause a complete and immediate loss of consciousness or impairment for the adversary.

As I said earlier, there's only two effective ways to apply incapacitation pressure points that causes a complete and immediate loss of consciousness for the adversary, impact

19

and blood flow pressure points. Let's take a quick look at each one.

Impact Pressure Points – these are vital and sensitive targets that can be struck. For example, knocking someone out with a power punch. Impact pressure points can also be struck with various hand held weapons, such as the tactical cane, kubotan, mini flashlight, combat stick, or club.

Pictured here, a short-arc hammer fist blow delivered to an impact pressure point target.

Blood Flow Pressure Points – when deliberate pressure is applied to these life sustaining targets, immediate unconsciousness and possible death can occur. As I stated previously, *blood flow pressure points should only be used in life and death situations that legally warrant the use of deadly force.*

For those of you who would like more information on Incapacitation Pressure Points, please see my book, *Combat Pressure Points.*

20

Pain Compliance Pressure Points

The second type of pressure point fighting method are *pain compliance techniques.* And for the purposes of this book, I'm going to focus exclusively on pain compliance pressure points that can be readily applied under real-world self-defense conditions.

Simply put, pain compliance pressure points are joint manipulation techniques used to gain immediate compliance from the adversary through the application of specific joint locks and holds.

These joint manipulation techniques can be used by anyone. But they're particularly useful for security personnel, law enforcement, and all types of low-level conflicts that don't justify knocking someone out. *The objective is to control and subdue an attacker with the least amount of physical force.*

Reasons for Using Pain Compliance Techniques

Here's a list of reasons why you should consider adding pain compliance techniques to your self-defense repertoire:

1. **Use of force** - self-defense is never a one technique solution. There are many situations that don't justify the use of extreme force. In such instances, you're legally and morally required to apply various nonlethal control techniques on the adversary.

2. **Nature of the beast** - in order for you to counter and escape any type of joint manipulation technique (remember, bad guys also study martial arts), you must first know how to apply it yourself.

3. **Occupational requirement** - some professions (police

21

officer, security guard, bouncer, bodyguard, etc.) require that you possess a working knowledge of various pain compliance techniques.

4. **Subduing a friend or relative** - in many cases, it's always best to restrain and control a friend or relative with a pain compliance technique instead of striking him.

5. **Anatomical orientation** - practicing various joint manipulation techniques will give you a greater understanding and appreciation of human anatomy and kinesiology.

6. **Psychological edge** - very few can argue the fact that a well executed pain compliance technique can psych-out your adversary as well as spectators observing the altercation.

When to Apply Pain Compliance Pressure Points?

Knowing *when* to apply pain compliance techniques is of critical importance for the self-defense practitioner. Keep in mind that applying a joint manipulation technique under the wrong self-defense conditions can be dangerous, and even deadly for you.

What follows is a list of ideal conditions for applying pain compliance techniques.

1. The adversary grabs hold of you.

2. You've stunned the adversary with a strike and must now control him.

3. Your occupation requires you to apply pain compliance techniques instead of striking.

4. You don't want to seriously injure the person threatening you (i.e., drunk friend, relative, emotionally disturbed person, etc).

When **NOT** to Apply Pain Compliance Techniques

Knowing when *not* to apply pain compliance techniques is just as important as knowing when to apply them. Here's a brief summary of when they should be avoided during a self-defense situation:

1. Under Immediate Attack - never apply pain compliance techniques when you're under immediate attack from the adversary. Remember, it's nearly impossible to apply pain compliance pressure points on your adversary when he's raining blows down on you.

2. Multiple assailants - since pain compliance pressure points require you to grab hold of the opponent's limb, it's virtually impossible to fight multiple attackers. If you want to survive such a perilous situation, you must abandon control techniques entirely and stick to impact techniques.

3. Edged weapon attacks - defending against a knife or edged weapon attack is incredibly dangerous. In order to survive, you must apply specific knife defense skills, not pain compliance techniques.

Pain compliance pressure points techniques must be avoided if you are going to survive a multiple attacker situation.

23

The Limitations of Pain Compliance Techniques

Although pain compliance pressure points are a necessary component of your combat cache, never forget their inherent risks and limitations. Here are just a few to keep in mind:

1. **Somatotype** - despite how proficient you might be with pain compliance techniques, many will not work effectively against large and anatomically hyper-flexible assailants.

2. **Assailant's size and strength** - these real-world factors can often negate the effectiveness of certain pain compliance holds.

3. **Psychoactive drugs** - many types of street drugs will make the adversary immune to pain… their effects will often nullify your pressure point compliance technique.

4. **Frenetic movements** - for any joint manipulation technique to work, you must have and maintain exact anatomical placement on your adversary. However, it's often very difficult to apply precise pain compliance techniques when the assailant is fueled by rage and adrenaline. In many cases, his actions will be riddled with broken rhythm and frenetic movements.

5. **Vulnerability** - pain compliance pressure points generally require you to apply them with both of your hands. This can leave you vulnerable if your adversary is able to strike you with his free hand.

Finally, pain compliance pressure points are just another tool in your self-defense toolkit. They are not a be-all and end-all self-defense solution. Just remember, use them judiciously and you'll come out on top.

CHAPTER TWO
The Wrists

WRIST LOCKS

In this chapter, I'm going to focus on the most fundamental pain compliance pressure point, the wrists. More specifically, the wrist lock. Essentially, a wrist lock is an extremely painful joint manipulation technique that requires you to attack the wrist-joint through rotation or flexion of the opponent's hand.

5 Ways to Attack the Opponent's Wrists

There are five ways that you can attack the opponent's wrists, and they include the following actions:

Flex-In - this is performed by flexing the opponent's palm inward towards his biceps.

Flex-Back - this requires you flex the back of the opponent's wrist towards his biceps.

Outside Twist - this requires you to twist the opponent's wrist towards the outside of his centerline.

Inside Twist - this is performed by twisting the opponent's wrist towards the inside of his centerline.

V-Pinch - this technique requires you to force an ulnar deviation on the opponent's hand.

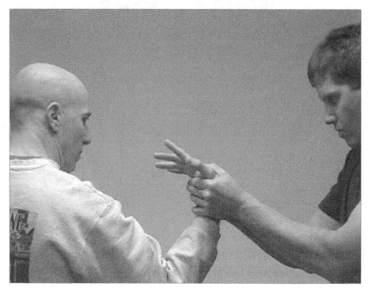

The Flex-In Wrist Lock

The Flex-Back Wrist Lock

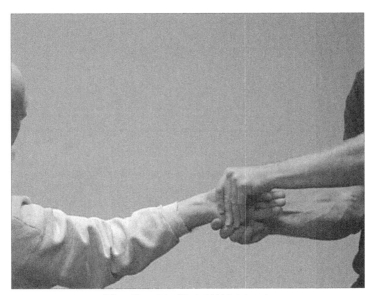

The Outside Twist Wrist Lock

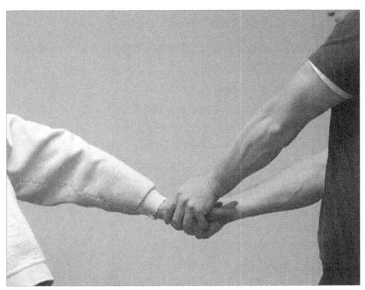

The Inside Twist Wrist Lock

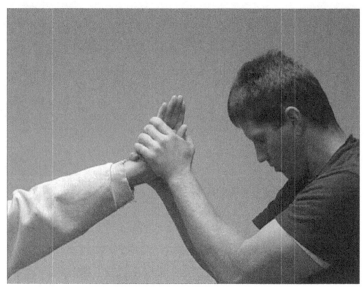

The V-Pinch Wrist Lock

Proactive and Reactive Wrist Locks

Essentially, there are two different types of wrist lock application scenarios, they include:

Reactive Wrist Locks - are performed when your adversary attacks you (in the form of a grab or hold), and you *react* and counter his assault with a wrist lock.

Proactive Wrist Locks - are performed when *you initiate* the wrist lock on your adversary. Proactive wrist locks are most often used by law enforcement and security personnel who must gain immediate compliance from the individual.

Reactive Wrist Lock Example

Step: 1

Step: 2

Step: 3

Step: 4

Proactive Wrist Lock Example

Step: 1

Step: 2

Step: 3

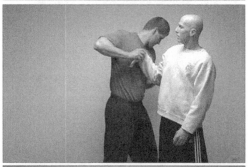

Step: 4

REACTIVE WRIST LOCKS

Here, I'm going to teach you all about reactive wrist locks. However, before moving forward, there's one critical caveat you must burn into your memory…

Whenever the adversary grabs hold of you, you must always raise your free hand up in a nonthreatening manner. This is what I refer to as the *proper set-up* for a successful pressure point wrist lock.

Raising your free hand prior to executing a wrist lock is a safety measure in the event your adversary initiates a strike.

PARTY FLEX WRIST LOCK
(Countering One-Hand Wrist Grab High)

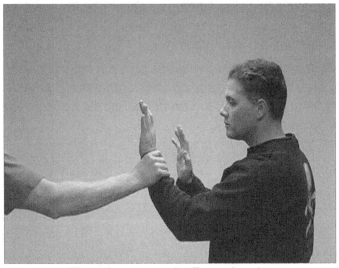

The adversary grabs Franco's wrist.

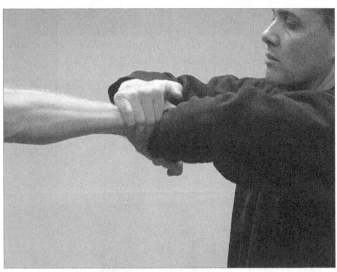

Franco's elevates his elbow sideways (so his arm is parallel to the ground) then grabs the edge of the assailant's hand.

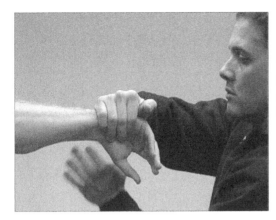

With the edge of the hand grasped firmly, Franco frees his hand by stripping it down.

Once his hand is free, he reaches under and grabs the top of the assailant's hand.

With Franco's thumbs placed side by side, he flexes the hand and wrist towards the opponent's body.

35

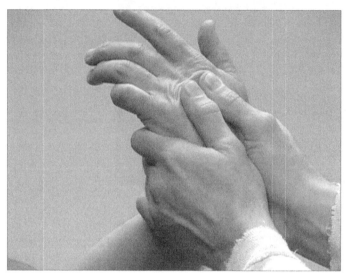

When performing the party flex wrist lock, be certain to keep both of your thumbs _below the opponent's knuckle line_. This will maximize the leverage on the opponent's wrist.

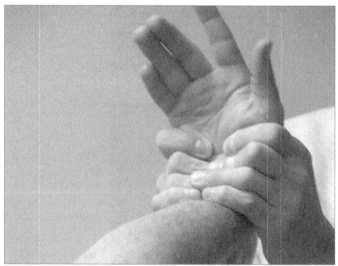

Pictured here, an inside view of the party flex wrist lock.

(Countering a Rear Pickpocket)

The pickpocket approaches.

He reaches inside the defender's rear pocket.

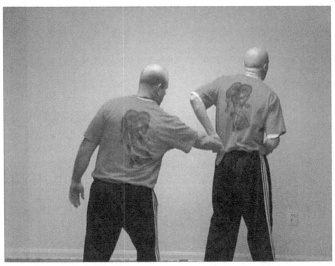

The defender reaches behind and grabs the assailant's hand.

He quickly spins around.

Without missing a beat. the defender forcefully applies the pain compliance hold.

The pickpocket is forced to the ground.

PARTY FLEX WRIST LOCK
(From the Mounted Position)

Wrist lock pressure points can also be applied when ground fighting with the adversary.

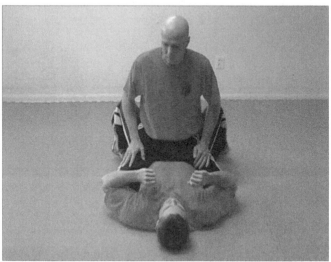

The practitioner begins from the top mounted position.

Before applying the pain compliance technique, the man on top stuns his adversary with a descending elbow strike.

40

He secures the opponent's elbow.

Next, he lowers his base and flexes the opponent's wrist to the ground.

41

ESCORT WRIST LOCK
(Countering One-Hand Wrist Grab High)

The adversary grabs Franco's wrist.

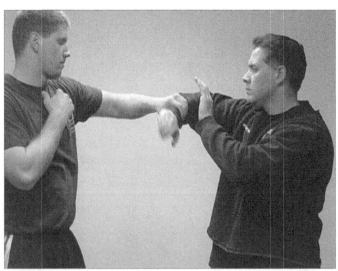

Franco's elevates his elbow sideways, so his arm is parallel to the ground.

With the edge of the hand grasped firmly, Franco frees his hand by stripping it down.

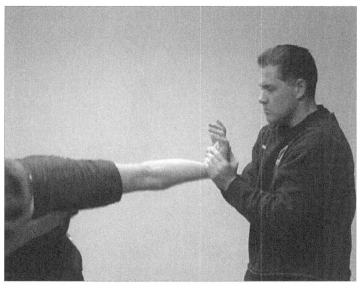

With Franco's thumbs placed side by side, he forcefully flexes the opponent's hand and wrist.

From the wrist lock position, Franco inserts his thumb between his opponent's thumb and index finger. He slaps his opponent's biceps upwards.

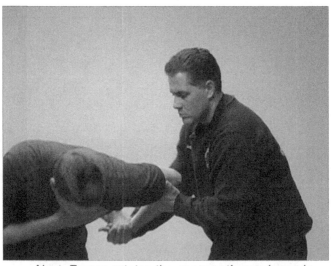

Next, Franco rotates the opponent's arm inwards.

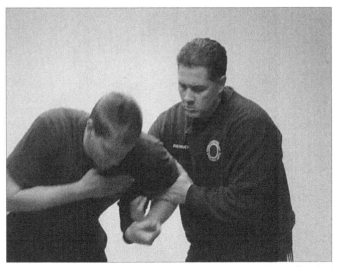

Franco steps in closer and inserts his opponent's elbow firmly into his chest region.

He maintains pressure on the opponent's wrist by turning it inwards.

45

Franco releases his hand from the opponent's biceps, and reinforces his other hand. If necessary, turn the opponent's wrist inward to apply more pressure.

PARTY FLEX WRIST LOCK
(Countering Two-Hand Wrist Grab High)

Franco assumes a de-escalation stance. His opponent grab both of his wrists.

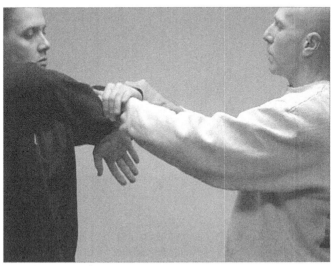

Franco's elevates his elbow sideways (so his arm is parallel to the ground) while simultaneously grabbing the edge of his opponent's hand.

47

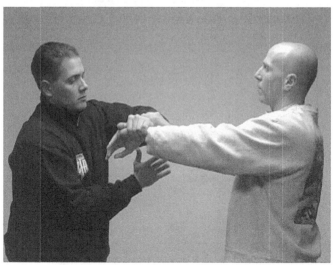

With the edge of the hand grasped firmly, Franco frees his hand by stripping it down.

Once his hand is free, Franco reaches under and grabs the top of the assailant's hand.

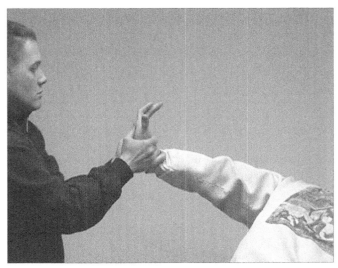

With Franco's thumbs placed side by side, he flexes the hand and wrist towards the opponent's body.

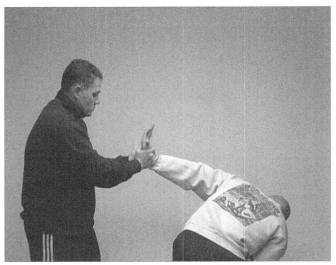

Franco applies more pressure, forcing his adversary to the ground.

PARTY FLEX WRIST LOCK
(Countering One-Hand Wrist Grab Low)

The opponent grabs the wrist.

The defender supinates his hand (palm up position).

The defender reaches under and grabs his opponent's wrist.

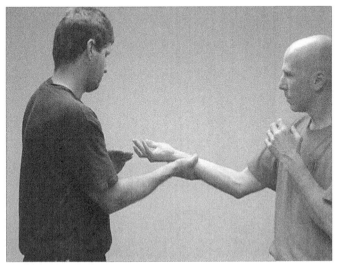

Next, the defender strips his hand free.

51

The defender grabs hold of the attacker's hand.

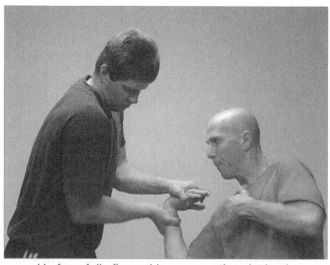

He forcefully flexes his opponent's wrist back.

OUTSIDE TWIST WRIST LOCK
(Countering One-Hand Wrist Grab Low)

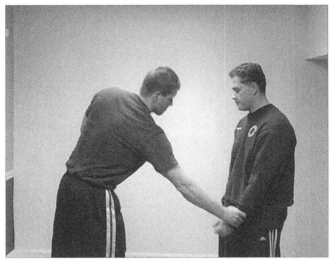

The adversary grabs Franco's wrist.

As a precaution against a possible punch, Franco raises his free hand.

Franco supinates his hand (palm up position).

Next, he reaches under and grabs the base of his opponent's thumb.

Franco strips his hand free from the opponent's grab.

With both hands held securely, Franco twists the opponent's wrist outward.

55

PARTY FLEX WRIST LOCK
(Countering Two-Hand Wrist Grab Low)

The adversary grabs both of Franco's wrists.

Franco supinates his left hand.

Franco reaches under and grabs the opponent's wrist.

Franco strips his hand free from the grab.

Next, he grabs his opponent's hand (excluding the thumb).

Franco forcefully flexes his opponent's wrist back.

V-PINCH WRIST LOCK
(Countering One-Hand Wrist Grab Low)

Franco is caught off guard with both hands down by his sides.

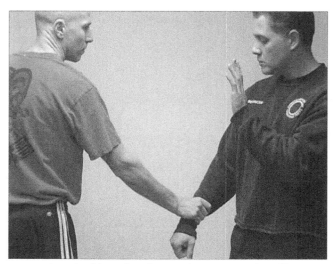

The opponent grabs his wrist. As a safety precaution, Franco raises his free hand up.

59

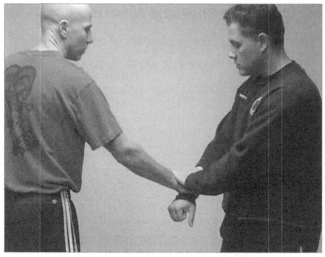

Next, Franco traps his opponent's grabbing hand against his own wrist.

With the opponent's hand trapped, Franco balls a fist and rotates his hand in a clockwise direction.

Franco forces his fist downward, causing a painful V-pinch in the opponent's wrist.

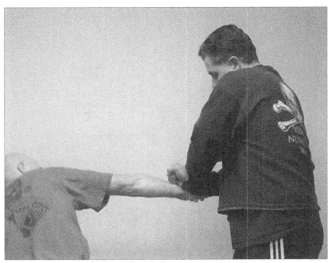

Franco forces his adversary to the ground.

V-PINCH WRIST LOCK
(Countering Two Hands On One)

Franco is caught off guard with both hands down by his sides.

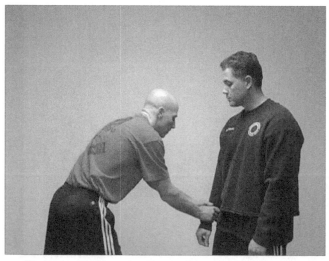

The adversary grabs Franco's wrist with both hands.

As a safety precaution, Franco raises his free hand up.

Next, Franco traps the opponent's wrist with his left hand.

63

With the opponent's hand trapped, Franco balls a fist and rotates his hand in a clockwise direction.

Franco forces his fist downward, causing a painful V-pinch in the opponent's wrist.

64

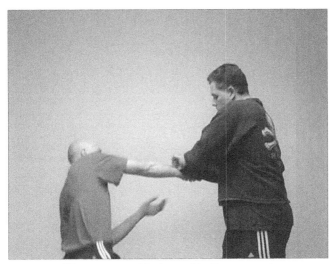

The opponent is forced to the ground.

PUNISHING PRESSURE POINTS

CHAPTER THREE
The Shoulders & Elbows

SHOULDER & ELBOW LOCKS

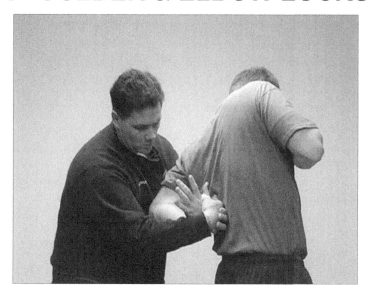

Now that you have a solid foundation of pressure point wrist locks, it's time to move on to the elbows and shoulders. In essence, I'm talking about arm locks that will either hyper-flex, hyperextend, or hyper-rotate the elbow or shoulder joint.

In this chapter, I'm going to cover a variety of shoulder and elbows locks performed in both the stand-up and ground fighting positions. Remember, all of these pressure point techniques are performed non-telegraphically and with lightning speed.

HAMMER LOCK
(Countering One-Hand Wrist Grab High)

Franco assumes a de-escalation stance. His opponent grab both of his wrists.

Franco swings his arm in a clockwise motion. This action bends the opponent's arm in a right angle.

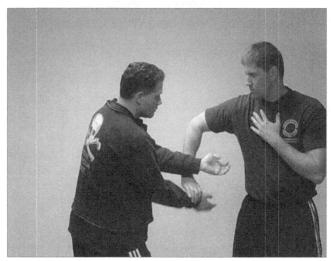

Next, Franco inserts his left arm against the opponent's inner forearm, and strips his right hand free from the grab.

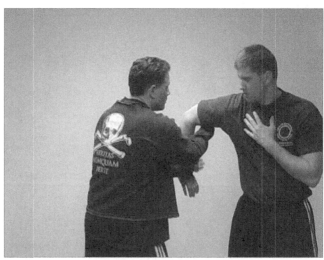

He pops his opponent's biceps upwards while bringing his arm backwards.

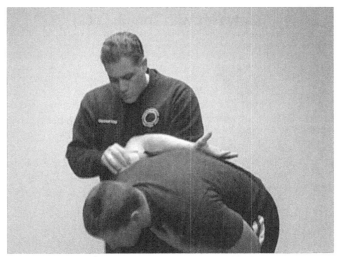

Franco quickly moves behind the adversary and bends the opponent's arm behind his back. The opponent's arm is now bent at a right angle with Franco's wrist leveraged inside the crook of his shoulder.

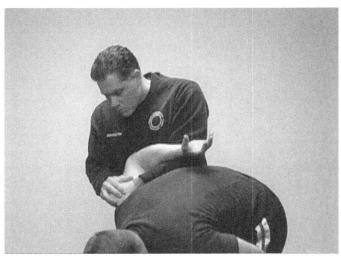

He maintains pressure on the shoulder while simultaneously elevating the opponent's wrist.

HAMMER LOCK
(Party Flex with Thumb Lock)

The opponent grabs the defenders wrist.

The defender swings his arm downward. This action bends the opponent's arm into a right angle.

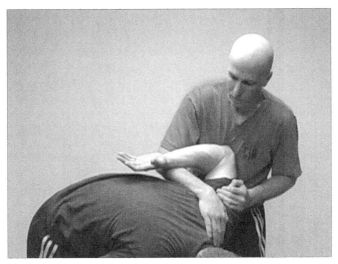

The defender pops his opponent's biceps upwards while bringing his arm backwards into the hammer lock position.

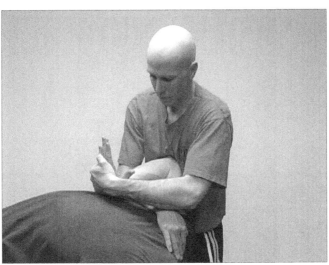

With the opponent's elbow secured against the lower chest, the defender simultaneously elevates the shoulder.

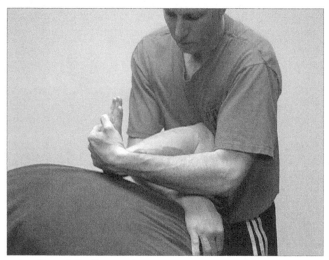

Next, he forcefully flexes the opponent's wrist towards his chest.

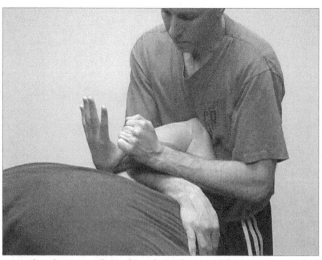

Another option is to apply a thumb lock, requiring you to grab the opponent's thumb and pull it backwards.

STANDING SHOULDER LIFT
(Countering a Shoulder Grab)

The assailant grabs Franco's left shoulder and prepares to launch an attack.

Franco swings his left arm around his opponent's arm and traps it securely under his armpit.

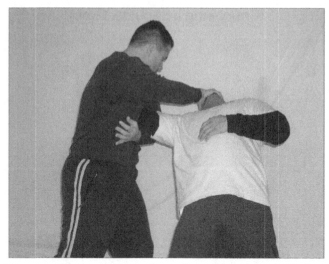

Franco counters with a palm strike to the opponent's face.

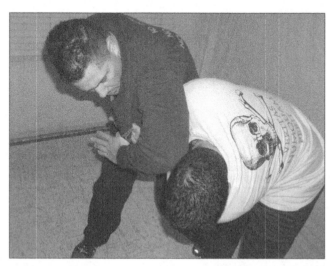

Next, he follows up with a diagonal elbow strike to the face.

SHOULDER CRANK
(From The Guard Position)

The defender has his opponent in his leg guard.

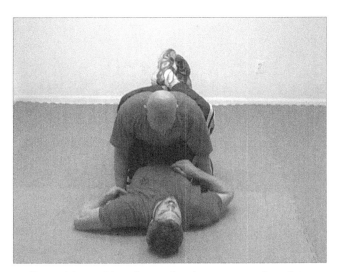

From this position, he grabs the opponent's wrist.

Next, he forces the opponent's arm back while simultaneously sitting up.

He bends the opponent's arm at a right angle and feeds his hand through it, making certain to grab his own wrist.

He slides his body out to the side, so the adversary falls forward.

With the shoulder crank held in place, he drives his elbow against the opponent's shoulder blade and slowly elevates his palm upward.

81

THE BOX
(From The Mounted Position)

Franco begins from the top mounted position.

He lowers his base, traps his opponent's arm to the ground while simultaneously bending it at a right angle.

Next, he slides his free arm under his opponent's trapped arm, and grasps his own wrist.

While securing the hold, Franco elevates the opponent's elbow and slowly drags it towards his legs.

WRIST LEVER
(From The Mounted Position)

Franco begins from the top mounted position.

He lowers his base and places his left elbow against the opponent's head.

84

Next, he reaches under the opponent's arm and grasps his wrist.

While pressing his elbow against the opponent's head, Franco elevates the opponent's elbow and drags it downward towards his legs.

85

SHOULDER CRUSH
(From The Mounted Position)

Franco begins from the top mounted position.

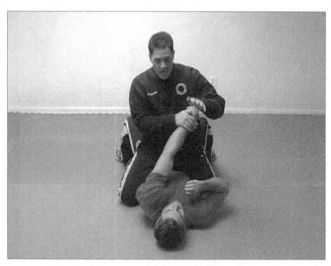

The adversary attempts a straight punch.

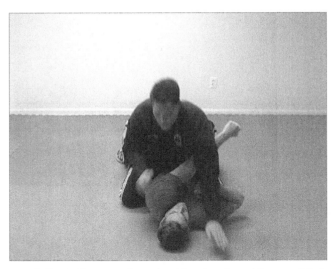

Franco deflects the punch under his armpit and lowers his base.

He slides his left arm under the opponent's neck.

87

Next, he grabs his own arm and lowers his head.

Franco grabs the opponent's forehead, lowers his bodyweight, forcing his chest against the opponent's trapped shoulder.

CHICKEN WING
(From The Side Mount Position)

From the side mount position, grab the opponent's closest arm.

Feed his arm between the crook of your bent knee.

89

Secure your leg behind your other leg, and tighten the gap between both of your thighs. Your adversary should not be able to move his arm. Next, clap your hands together using an Indian grip.

Once your legs and arms are tight and secure, slowly thrust your hips forward to gain compliance from your adversary.

SINGLE ELBOW BREAK
(From The Guard Position)

Begin with the adversary in your leg guard.

The man on the bottom reaches across and traps both of the opponent's arms. Next, he simultaneously leverages his right leg against the opponent's left elbow.

91

Warning! Remember to always trap both of your opponent's arms when performing this pressure point technique.

As seen in this photo, failure to trap both of the opponent's arms can lead to big problems for the man on the bottom.

DOUBLE ELBOW BREAK
(From The Guard Position)

Begin with the adversary in your leg guard.

Trap both of the opponent's arms against your chest, and quickly open your leg guard.

Place both of your ankles against the sides of the opponent's neck.

With the opponent's arms held securely, raise both of your hips upward, forcing pressure against both of his elbows.

JAPANESE ARM BAR
(From The Guard Position)

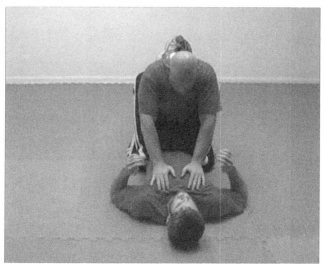

Begin with the adversary in your leg guard.

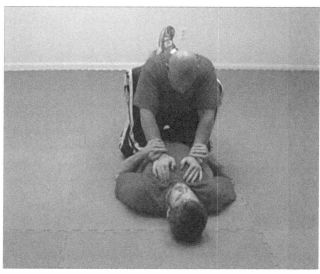

Trap both of the opponent's arms against your chest.

95

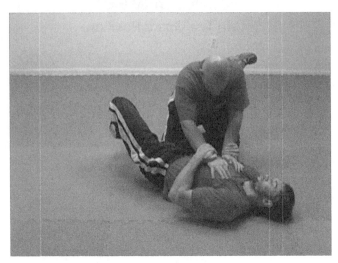

While trapping the opponent's arms, quickly pivot your hips to the right.

Swing your left leg over the opponent's shoulder.

96

Grab the opponent's right arm with both of your hands, and force the opponent on his back.

Trap the opponent's wrist against your chest while simultaneously elevating your hips upwards.

97

ELBOW COMPRESSION
(Countering a Rear Collar Grab)

Franco is grabbed from behind.

He breaks the opponent's grab by stepping forward and circling his left arm around both his opponent's arms.

With both of the opponent's arms trapped, Franco counterattacks
with an eye rake.

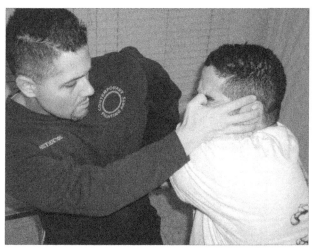

Notice how Franco maintains control of his assailant's arms while
executing the eye rake.

STRAIGHT ARM BAR
(From The Mounted Position)

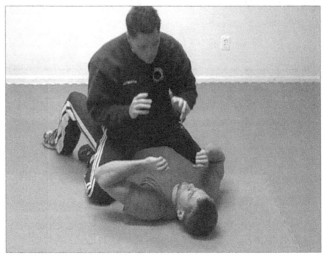

Franco begins from the top mounted position.

He lowers his base, traps his opponent's arm to the ground.

The opponent resists Franco and stretches his arm outward. Franco sees the opening and slides his right arm under the opponent's elbow.

Next, Franco grabs his own forearm while realigning the opponent's wrist (opponent's thumb should be pointing upwards). Pain compliance is gained by simply rolling your wrist upward against the opponent's elbow.

101

ARM BAR OVER LEG
(From The Side Mount Position)

From the side mount position, grab the opponent's closest arm.

Next, switch leg positions (bring your rear leg forward and front leg back).

102

*With your leg braced firmly against the ground, place the opponent's
elbow over your thigh.*

*Pain compliance is gained by pushing the opponent's elbow against
your leg.*

103

CHAPTER FOUR
Pressure Point Takedowns

THE TAKEDOWN

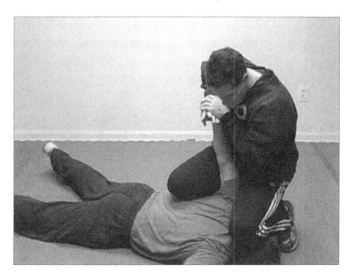

We've covered a variety of wrist, shoulder and elbow pressure point techniques. Now, I'm going to show you how to take the opponent down to the ground once you've successfully applied your pain compliance technique.

PARTY FLEX TAKEDOWN
(Countering One-Hand Wrist Grab High)

The adversary grabs Franco's wrist.

Franco's raises his elbow sideways, so his arm is parallel to the ground.

Next, he grabs the edge of the opponent's hand.

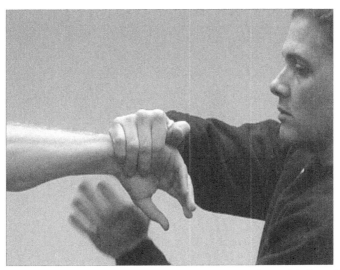

With the edge of the hand grasped firmly, Franco frees his hand by stripping it down.

With Franco's thumbs placed side by side, he flexes the opponent's hand and wrist.

With the opponent's wrist held close to Franco's chest, he applies downward pressure on the pressure point.

110

Franco barks out the command "down!" "down!" "down!" as he forces the adversary to the ground.

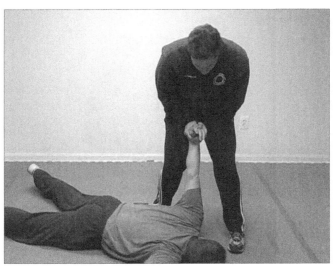

Compliance is gained by flexing the opponent's wrist and shoulder downward.

111

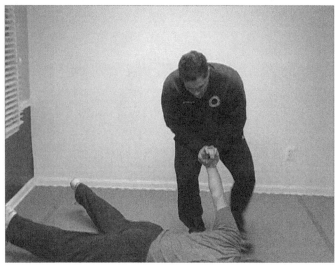

While maintaining pressure on both the opponent's wrist and shoulder, Franco kneels down.

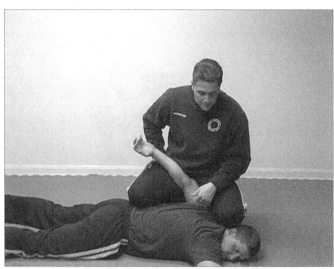

Franco supports himself on the opponent's back and upper shoulder, establishing the standard "handcuff position." This is a temporary position that should only be held for a short period of time.

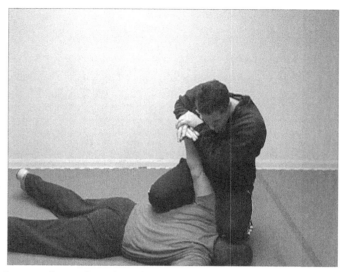

Pain compliance is gained by simply flexing the opponent's wrists.

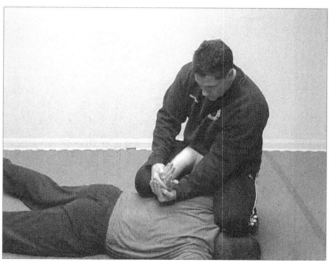

If necessary, you can flex the opponent's wrist and elbow in a variety of different angles to gain further compliance.

113

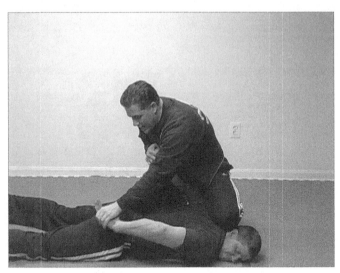

Franco orders his adversary to give him his other hand.

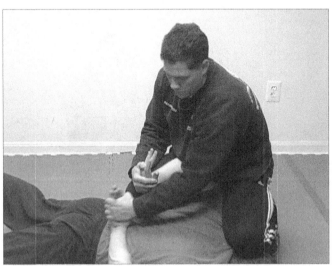

Both of the opponent's hands are now in Franco's control.

PARTY FLEX TAKEDOWN VARIATION
(Countering One-Hand Wrist Grab Low)

The opponent grabs the defender's wrist.

The defender raises his free hand.

115

Next, he supinates his hand, reaches under, and grabs the opponent's wrist.

The defender grabs hold of the attacker's hand, and flexes his wrist back.

The defender barks out the command "down!" "down!" "down!" as he forces his opponent to the ground.

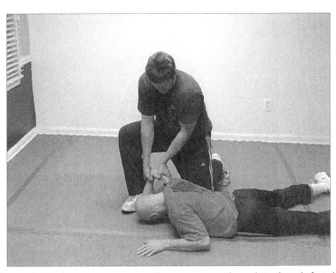

While maintaining pressure on the opponent's wrist, the defender kneels down.

117

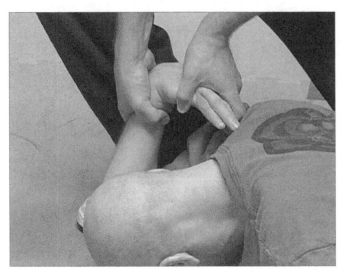

Picture here, close up view of the wrist lock.

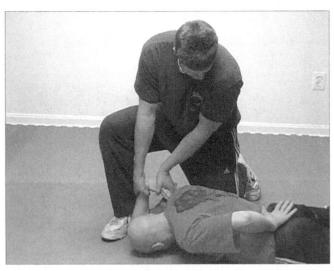

Once the pressure point technique is in place, the defender orders the adversary to put his other hand behind his back.

118

PARTY FLEX TAKEDOWN VARIATION
(Countering Two-Hand Wrist Grab Low)

The adversary grabs both of the defender's wrists.

The defender supinates his left hand.

Next, he reaches under and grabs the opponent's wrist.

The defender strips his hand free from the grab, and grabs his opponent's hand (excluding the thumb).

120

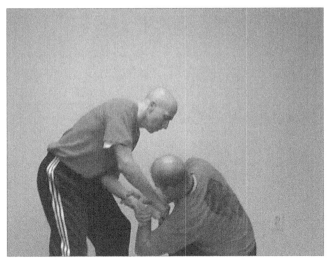

The defender flexes the opponent's wrist, while barking out the command "down!" "down!" "down!"

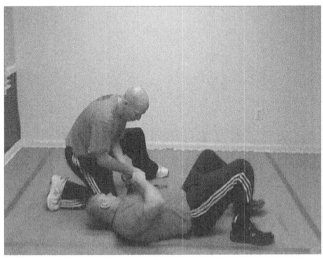

The opponent is forced to the ground.

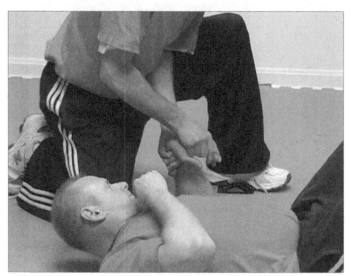

Pictured here, close up view of the wrist lock.

OUTSIDE TWIST TAKEDOWN
(Countering One-Hand Wrist Grab Low)

The opponent grabs Franco's wrist.

As a precaution against a possible punch, Franco raises his free hand.

123

Franco supinates his hand (palm up position).

He reaches under and grabs the base of his opponent's thumb.

He strips his hand free from the opponent's grab.

With both hands held securely, Franco forcefully twists the opponent's wrist outward.

125

Franco barks out the command "down!" "down!" "down!" as he forces the adversary to the ground.

Franco maintains pressure on the wrist as the opponent falls on his back.

126

V-PINCH TAKEDOWN
(Counter One-Hand Wrist Grab Low-Opposite Side)

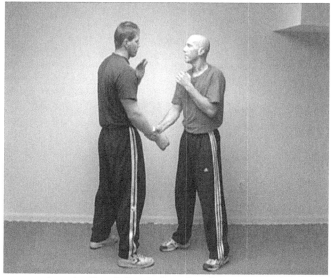

The opponent grabs the defender's wrist. As a precaution against a possible punch, the defender raises his free hand.

The defender traps his opponent's grabbing hand against his wrist.

127

With the opponent's hand trapped, the defender balls a fist and rotates his hand in a clockwise direction.

Next, he forces his fist downward, causing a painful V-pinch in the opponent's wrist.

While maintaining pressure on the opponent's wrist, the defender barks out the command "down!" "down!" "down!"

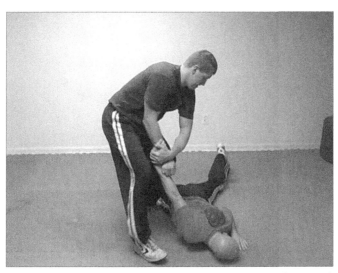

With the adversary flat on his stomach, the takedown is complete.

129

OTHER TAKEDOWN METHODS
(Using Handcuffs)

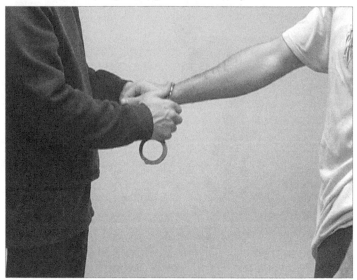

If you're involved with law enforcement or security work, you can also apply pain compliance holds with a handcuff.

Franco places both of his thumbs against the double strand of the closed handcuff.

Next, he forces the double strand (top metal portion of the handcuff) into the top portion of the opponent's wrist.

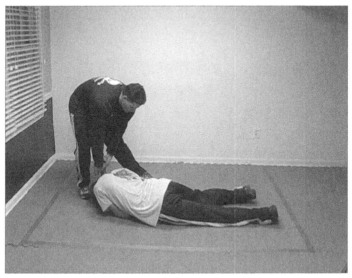

Franco barks out the command "down!" "down!" "down!" as he forces the adversary to the ground.

OTHER TAKEDOWN METHODS
(Using the Kubotan)

The kubotan is another effective tool for taking the opponent down to the ground. Here, the adversary grabs Franco by his shirt.

Franco places the long portion of the kubotan across the top of the opponent's wrist. He secures the position by placing both of his thumbs under the bottom portion of the adversary's wrist.

132

Next, he squeezes the kubotan firmly against the opponent's wrist while barking out the command "down!" "down!" "down!"

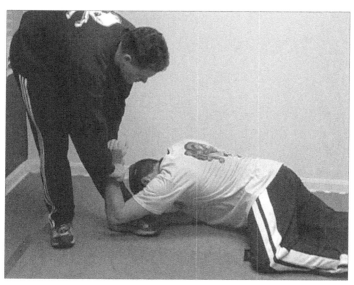

The adversary is taken to the ground.

CHAPTER FIVE
Pressure Point Drills

AWARENESS DRILLS

The drills featured in this chapter are designed to sharpen your awareness of possible attacks when performing various pain compliance pressure point techniques. They're also an essential component of joint manipulation proficiency and should be practiced on a regular basis with a trustworthy partner.

We're going to start with a basic punching awareness drill and work our way into knife defense. Keep in mind, all of these drills can be performed both with and without full-contact gear.

Step: 1

Step: 2

Step: 3

Step: 4

Step: 5

Step: 6

Step: 1

Step: 2

Step: 3

140

Step: 4

Step: 5

Step: 6

141

Step: 1

Step: 2

Step: 3

Step: 4

Step: 5

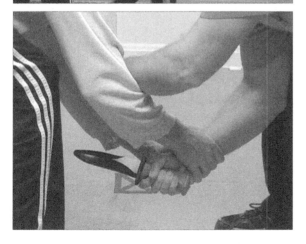

Step: 6

143

Step: 1

Step: 2

Step: 3

Step: 4

Step: 5

Step: 6

Step: 1

Step: 2

Step: 3

Step: 4

Step: 5

Step: 6

Step: 1

Step: 2

Step: 3

FLOW DRILLS

Pressure point techniques can also be developed through flow drills. Flow drills are excellent for developing both speed and reaction time. Here are a few examples to get you started.

Step 1: The two men begin the flow drill with the man on the right initiating a tight overhead strike. The man on the left blocks the hit.

Step 2: After blocking the strike, the man (left) uses his right arm to redirect his partner's striking arm.

Step 3: As the man on the left redirects his partner's arm, he slaps it downward with his left hand.

Step 4: Next, the man on the left attacks his partner with a tight overhead strike.

151

Step 5: The man on the right blocks his partner's strike and redirects it with his arm.

Step 6: As he redirects his partner's arm, he slaps it downward with his left hand.

Step 7: The cycle is complete and the man on the right begins again with a tight overhead strike. The drill continues back and forth.

INTEGRATING PRESSURE POINTS

Next, we're going to integrate pain compliance pressure points within the flow drill. This action is done arbitrarily between the training partners. Remember, always strive to keep the drill fluid and alive.

153

Step: 1

Step: 2

Step: 3

Step: 4

Step: 5

Step: 6

155

Step: 7

Step: 8

Step: 9

Step: 10

Step: 11

Step: 12

Step: 13

Step: 14

Step: 15

Step: 16

Step: 17

Step: 18

159

Step: 19

Step: 20

Step: 21

Step: 22

Step: 23

Step: 24

Step: 25

Step: 26

TWO-HANDS LOW DRILL

This drill teaches you how to choose and apply the proper wrist lock technique when grabbed from a low hand position.

This drill requires you to hold both hands by the sides of your body (in the event you're caught off guard by an approaching individual). From this starting point, your training partner arbitrarily grabs either hand (either cross grab or mirror image), forcing you to execute a split-second pressure point technique.

163

Step: 1

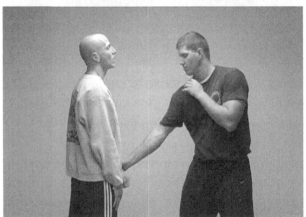

Step: 2

Step: 3

Step: 4

Step: 5

Step: 6

165

Step: 7

Step: 8

Step: 9

Step: 10

Step: 11

Step: 12

167

Step: 13

Step: 14

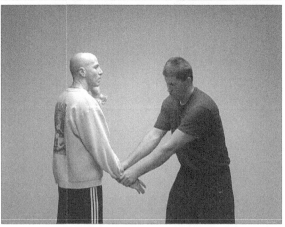

Step: 15

Step: 16

Step: 17

Step: 18

HIGH-LOW SPEED DRILL

This advanced pressure point drill teaches you how to quickly choose and apply the proper wrist lock technique for just about any type of grab.

This speed drill requires you to hold one hand high, and the other one low. From this starting point, your partner arbitrarily grabs either hand (cross grab or mirror image), forcing you to make a split-second decision.

Step: 1

Step: 2

Step: 3

Step: 4

Step: 5

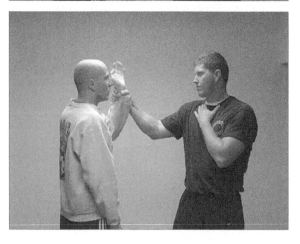

Step: 6

Step: 7

Step: 8

Step: 9

173

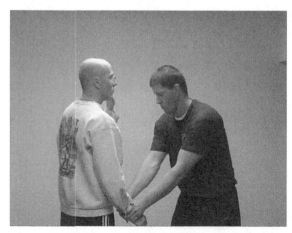

Step: 10

Step: 11

Step: 12

Step: 13

Step: 14

Step: 15

175

Step: 16

Step: 17

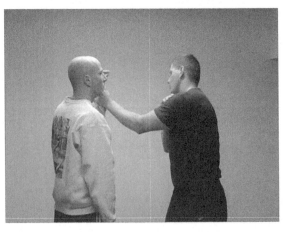

Step: 18

Step: 19

Step: 20

Step: 21

CHAPTER SIX
Additional Pressure Points

BONUS PRESSURE POINT TECHNIQUES

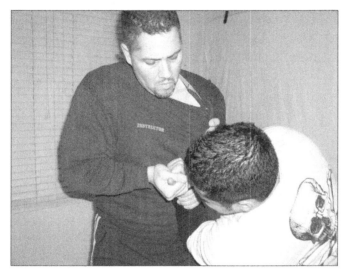

There are other pain compliance pressure point techniques that don't fall under the category of joint manipulation. However, they're very effective and can be readily applied under the stress of an emergency self-defense situation. Here are just a few to get you started.

THE FINGERS

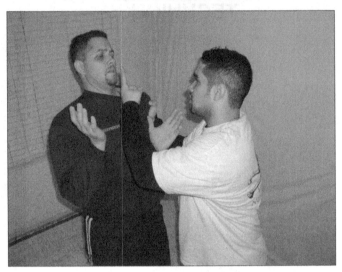

The assailant grabs Franco's shirt and sticks his finger in is face.

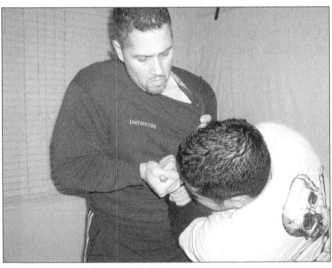

Franco grabs hold of his opponent's wrist and simultaneously breaks his index finger.

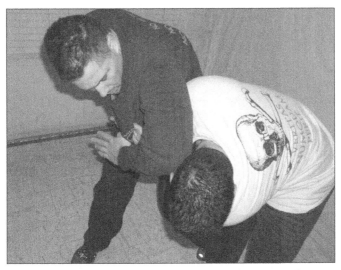

He quickly follows up with a diagonal elbow strike.

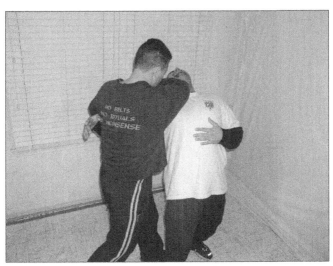

Franco completes his assault with another elbow strike.

183

Franco is grabbed from behind.

To prevent himself from being lifted, Franco bumps his hips back and repeatedly smashes his opponent's hands with his knuckles.

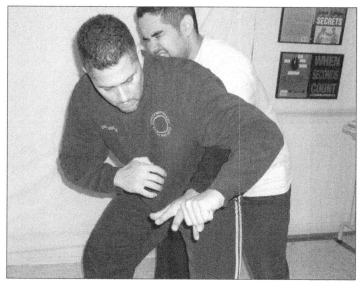

Once his adversary loosens his grip, Franco snatches his finger and breaks it.

Franco spins his body out of the hold.

185

Franco is choked from behind.

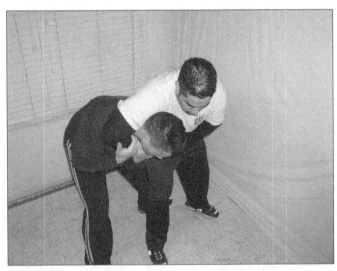

He grabs hold of his opponent's arm and stabilizes his balance.
Next, Franco steps behind his adversary and turns his head inward.

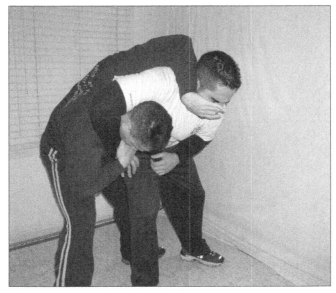

Franco reaches from behind and places his middle finger under his opponent's septum.

He forcefully pulls his adversary backwards.

187

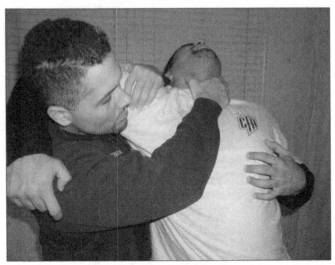

Franco attacks the throat. Remember, attacking the assailant's throat must only be used when lethal force is warranted and justified in the eyes of the law.

CHAPTER SEVEN
Strengthening Exercises

STRENGTHENING EXERCISES

There are several exercises you can use to help condition and strengthen your wrists and forearms for the rigors of joint manipulation pressure point techniques.

We're going to start with a basic flexibility exercise that helps warm up and loosen the muscles, tendons and ligaments of the wrists and forearms.

191

HELICOPTERS

Step: 1

Step: 2

Step: 3

STICK TWIRLS

Step: 1

Step: 2

Step: 3

GRIP STRENGTH

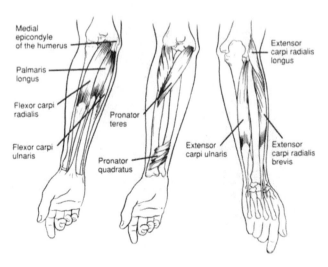

Now that we've covered warm up exercises, it's time to talk about grip strength.

Grip strength is a vital component of pressure point fighting. In fact, powerful hands and forearms will also amplify the speed and power of your joint manipulation techniques.

Most importantly, strong forearms will dramatically enhance your wrist manipulation skills and enhance your ability to control the assailant's limbs from a variety of positions.

There are several effective hand and forearm exercises you can perform at your leisure to strengthen these important muscles. What follows are several efficient ways to condition and strengthen your hands, wrists and forearms. Try to perform these exercise at least twice per week.

TENNIS BALL

If you're low on cash and just starting out with your training, you can start by squeezing a tennis ball a couple times per week. One hundred repetitions per hand would be a great start.

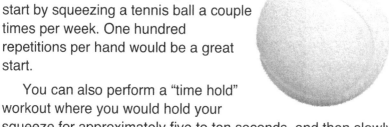

You can also perform a "time hold" workout where you would hold your squeeze for approximately five to ten seconds, and then slowly release the pressure. You would repeat this process anywhere from 10 to 15 repetitions. Next, switch the ball to your other hand and start over. Sounds easy? I can assure you, it's not!

POWER PUTTY

One excellent hand exerciser that strengthens all the muscles in your fingers and hands is Power Putty. Essentially, Power Putty is a flexible silicone rubber that can be squeezed, stretched, and crushed. Begin using the putty for ten minute sessions and progressively build up to thirty minutes.

This tough resistant putty will strengthen the muscles of your forearm, wrists, hands and fingers. Remember to work both hands equally.

195

IRON MIND EGG

This is another great tool for strengthening and conditioning your hands for the demands of joint manipulation techniques. Made of a 21st century polymer, the Iron Mind EGG will add a new dimension to your grip training.

HAND GRIPPERS

Another effective way to strengthen your hands, wrists and forearms is to work out with heavy duty hand grippers. While there are a wide selection of them on the market, I personally prefer using the Captains of Crush brand.

These high quality grippers are virtually indestructible and they are sold in a variety of different resistance levels ranging from 60 to 365 pounds. They're the best money can buy!

196

WEIGHT TRAINING

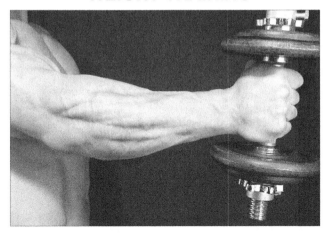

Finally, you can condition your wrists and forearms by performing various forearm exercises with free weights.

Exercises like hammer curls, reverse curls, wrist curls, and reverse wrist curls are great for developing powerful forearms.

When training your forearms, be certain to work both your extensor and flexor muscles. Let's look at some of the exercises.

BARBELL WRIST CURLS

This exercise strengthens the flexor muscles. Perform 5 sets of 10-12 repetitions. To perform the exercise, follow these steps:

1. Sit at the end of a bench, grab a barbell with an underhand grip and place both of your hands close together.

2. In a smooth and controlled fashion, slowly bend your wrists and lower the barbell toward the floor. The slower, the better.

3. Contract your forearms and curl the weight back to the starting position.

4. Perform this exercise at least twice per week.

REVERSE WRIST CURLS

This exercise develops and strengthens the extensor muscle of the forearm. Perform 5 sets of 10-12 repetitions. To perform the exercise, follow these steps:

1. While standing, hold a barbell with an overhand grip, with your hands approximately chest width apart.

2. Slowly lower the barbell as far as your wrists will allow.

3. Flex your wrists upward back to the starting position.

4. Perform this exercise at least twice per week.

HAMMER CURLS

This exercise strengthens both the Brachialis and Brachioradialis muscles. To perform the exercise, follow these steps:

1. Stand with both feet approximately shoulder width apart, with both dumbbells at your sides.

2. Keeping your elbows close to your body and your palms facing inward, slowly curl both dumbbells upward towards your shoulders.

3. Slowly return to the starting position.

4. Perform 5 sets of 12-15 reps at least twice per week.

GENERAL COMBAT CONDITIONING

Finally, if you want to maximize the efficiency and effectiveness of your clinch fighting skills, you must be physically fit. Fitness and conditioning comprises the following three broad components: cardiorespiratory conditioning, muscular/ skeletal conditioning, and proper body composition.

The cardiorespiratory system includes the heart, lungs, and circulatory system, which undergo tremendous stress in a high-risk situation. So you're going to have to run, jog, bike, swim, or skip rope to develop sound cardiorespiratory conditioning. Each aerobic workout should last a minimum of 30 minutes and be performed at least four times per week.

The second component of conditioning is muscular/skeletal conditioning. To strengthen your bones and muscles to withstand the rigors of combat, your training must include progressive resistance (weight training). You will also need a stretching program designed to loosen up every muscle group. As I said earlier, stretching on a regular basis will also increase the muscles' range of motion, improve circulation, reduce the possibility of injury and relieve daily stress.

The final component of conditioning is proper body composition: simply, the ratio of fat to lean body tissue. Your diet and training regimen will affect your level or percentage of body fat significantly. A sensible and consistent exercise program accompanied by a healthy and balanced diet will facilitate proper body composition.

Glossary

A

Accuracy - The precise or exact projection of force. Accuracy is also defined as the ability to execute a combative movement with precision and exactness.

Action - A series of moving parts that permit a firearm to be loaded, unloaded and fired.

Adaptability - The ability to physically and psychologically adjust to new or different conditions or circumstances of combat.

Aerobic Exercise - "With air." Exercise that elevates the heart rate to a training level for a prolonged period of time, usually 30 minutes.

Affective Domain - This includes the attitudes, philosophies, ethics, values, discretionary use-of-force, and the spirit (killer instinct) required to use your combative tool or technique appropriately.

Affective Preparedness - Being emotionally and spiritually prepared for the demands and strains of combat.

Aggression - Hostile and injurious behavior directed toward a person.

Aggressive Hand Positioning - Placement of hands so as to imply aggressive or hostile intentions.

Aggressive Stance - (See Fighting Stance.)

Aggressor - One who commits an act of aggression.

Agility - An attribute of combat. One's ability to move his or her body quickly and gracefully.

Amalgamation - A scientific process of uniting or merging.

Ambidextrous - The ability to perform with equal facility on both the right and left sides of the body.

Ambush - To lie in wait and attack by surprise.

Ambush Zones - Strategic locations (in everyday environments) from which assailants launch surprise attacks.

American Stick Strangle - A stick strangle used with a hammer grip.

Analysis and Integration - One of the five elements of CFA's mental component. This is the painstaking process of breaking down various elements, concepts, sciences, and disciplines into their atomic parts, and then methodically and strategically analyzing, experimenting, and drastically modifying the information so that it fulfills three combative requirements: efficiency, effectiveness and safety. Only then is it finally integrated into the CFA system.

Anatomical Handles - Various body parts (i.e., appendages, joints, and in some cases, organs) that can be grabbed, held, pulled or otherwise manipulated during a ground fight.

Anatomical Power Generators - Three points on the human body that help torque your body to generate impact power. Anatomical Power Generators include: (1) Feet; (2) Hips; (3) Shoulders.

Anatomical Striking Targets - The various anatomical body targets that can be struck and which are especially vulnerable to potential harm. They include: the eyes, temple, nose, chin, back of neck, front of neck, solar plexus, ribs, groin, thighs, knees, shins, and instep.

Arm Lock - A joint lock applied to the arm.

Assailant - A person who threatens or attacks another.

Assault - The willful attempt or threat to inflict injury upon the person of another.

Assault and Battery - The unlawful touching of another person without justification.

Assert - One of the five possible tactical responses to a threatening situation. To stand up for your rights (see Comply, Escape, De-Escalate, and Fight Back).

Assessment - The process of rapidly gathering, analyzing, and accurately evaluating information in terms of threat and danger. You can assess people, places, actions, and objects.

Attachment - The touching of the arms or legs prior to executing a trapping technique.

Attack - Offensive action designed to physically control, injure, or kill another person.

Attack By Draw - One of the five conventional methods of attack. A method of attack whereby the fighter offers his assailant an intentional opening designed to lure an attack.

Attributes of Combat - The physical, mental, and spiritual qualities that enhance combat skills and tactics.

Attribute Uniformity - Various combative attributes (i.e., speed, power, accuracy, balance, etc.) which are executed the same way every time.

Autoloader - A handgun that operates by mechanical spring pressure and recoil force that ejects the spent cartridge case and automatically feeds a fresh round from the magazine. (Also known as a Semiautomatic).

Awareness - Perception or knowledge of people, places, actions, and objects. (In CFA there are three categories of tactical awareness: Criminal Awareness, Situational Awareness, and Self-Awareness.)

Axiom - A truth that is self-evident.

B

Back Position - One of the ground fighting positions. The back position is assumed when your chest is on top of your assailant's back.

Back fist - A punch made with the back of the knuckles.

Back strap - The rear, vertical portion of the pistol frame.

Balance - One's ability to maintain equilibrium while stationary or moving.

Barrier - Any large object that can be used to obstruct an attacker's path or angle of attack.

Blading the Body - Strategically positioning your body at a 45-degree angle.

Block - A defensive tool designed to intercept the assailant's attack by placing a non-vital target between the assailant's strike and your vital body target.

Bludgeon - Any club like weapon used for offensive and defensive purposes (e.g., baseball bat, club, pipe, crowbar, heavy tree branch, etc.) Bludgeons are usually heavier and thicker than sticks.

Body Composition - The ratio of fat to lean body tissue.

Body Language - Nonverbal communication through posture, gestures, and facial expressions.

Body Mechanics - Technically precise body movement during the execution of a body weapon, defensive technique, or other fighting maneuver.

Body Weapon - One of the various body parts that can be used to strike or otherwise injure or kill a criminal assailant. (Also known as Tool).

Bore - The inside of the barrel of a firearm.

Boxing - (See Western Boxing).

Break fall - A method of safely falling to the ground.

Burn Out - A negative emotional state acquired by physically over training. Some symptoms of burn-out include: physical illness, boredom, anxiety, disinterest in training, and general sluggish behavior.

Bushido - The ancient and honorable code of the samurai

or warrior.

C

Cadence - Coordinating tempo and rhythm to establish a timing pattern of movement.

Caliber - The diameter of a projectile.

Cardiorespiratory Conditioning - A component of physical fitness that deals with the heart, lungs, and circulatory system.

Carriage - The way you carry yourself.

Cartridge - A cylindrical case containing components of a round of ammunition: case, primer, powder charge, and bullet.

Center-Fire - A type of firearm cartridge that has its primer located in the center of the case bottom.

Centerline - An imaginary vertical line that divides your body in half and which contains many of your vital anatomical targets.

Center Mass - The center portion of the torso.

Chamber - 1) The part of a firearm in which a cartridge is contained at the instant of firing. 2) The raising of the knee to execute a kick.

Choice Words - (See Selective Semantics.)

Choke - A close quarter (grappling range) technique that requires one to apply pressure to either the trachea of carotid arteries.

Circular Movement - Movements that follow the direction of a curve.

Close Quarter Combat - One of the three ranges of knife and bludgeon combat. At this distance, you can strike, slash, or stab your assailant with a variety of close-quarter techniques.

Close to Contact Shooting - Discharging a firearm with the muzzle approximately one inch distance from the target.

Cognitive Development - One of the five elements of CFA's mental component. The process of developing and enhancing your fighting skills through specific mental exercises and techniques. (see Analysis and Integration, Killer Instinct, Philosophy and Strategic/Tactical Development.)

Cognitive Domain - This encompasses the specific concepts, principles and knowledge required to use your combative tools or techniques effectively.

Cognitive Exercises - Various mental exercises used to enhance fighting skills and tactics.

Combat Arts - The various arts of war. (See Martial Arts.) Combative Attributes - (See Attributes.)

Combative Fitness - A state characterized by cardiorespiratory and muscular/ skeletal conditioning, as well as proper body composition.

Combative Mentality - A combative state of mind necessary for fighting. Also known as the Killer Instinct. (see Killer Instinct.)

Combat Ranges - The various ranges of armed and unarmed combat.

Combative Power - The ability of capacity to perform or act effectively in combat.

Combative Truth - A combative element that conforms to fact or actuality and which is proven to be true.

Combative Utility - The quality of condition of being combatively useful. Combination(s) - (See Compound Attack.)

Come-Along - A series of holds or joint locks that force your adversary to move in any direction you desire.

Coming to a Base - The process of getting up to your hands and knees from the prone position.

Common Peroneal Nerve - A pressure point area located approximately four to six inches above the knee on the midline of the outside of the thigh.

Completion Phase - One of the three stages of a stick or bludgeon strike. The completion phase is the completion point of a swing.

Comply - One of the five tactical responses to a threatening situation. To obey an assailant's demands. (see Assert, De-Escalate, Escape, and Fight Back.)

Composure - A combative attribute. Composure is a quiet and focused mind set that enables you to acquire your combative agenda.

Compound Attack - One of the five conventional methods of attack. Two or more body weapons launched in strategic succession whereby the fighter overwhelms his assailant with a flurry of full speed, full force blows. (see Indirect Attack, Immobilization Attack, Attack By Draw, and Single Attack.)

Concealment - Not being visible to your adversary.

Conditioning Training - A CFA training methodology requiring the practitioner to deliver a variety of offensive and defensive combinations for a four minute period (see Proficiency Training and Street Training.)

Confrontation Evasion - Strategically manipulating the distance or environment to avoid a possible confrontation.

Congruency - The state of harmoniously orchestrating the verbal and non verbal de-escalation principles.

Contact Evasion - Physically moving or manipulating your body targets to avoid being struck (i.e., slipping your head to the side or side stepping from a charging assailant).

Contact Shooting - Discharging a firearm with the muzzle touching the target.

Contemporary Fighting Arts® (CFA) - A modern martial art and self-defense system made up of three parts: physical, mental, and spiritual.

Conventional Ground Fighting Tools - Specific ground fighting techniques designed to control, restrain and temporarily incapacitate your adversary. Some conventional ground fighting tactics include: submission holds, locks, certain choking techniques, and specific striking techniques.

Cool-down - A series of light exercises and movements that immediately follow a workout. The purpose of the cool-down is to hasten the removal of metabolic wastes and gradually return the heart to its resting rate.

Coordination - A physical attribute characterized by the ability to perform a technique or movement with efficiency, balance, and accuracy.

Counterattack - Offensive action made to counter an assailant's initial attack.

Courage - A combative attribute. The state of mind and spirit that enables a fighter to face danger and vicissitudes with confidence, resolution, and bravery.

Courageousness - (See Courage).

Cover - Any object that protects you from gunfire.

Criminal Awareness - One of the three categories of CFA awareness. It involves a general understanding and knowledge of the nature and dynamics of a criminal's motivations, mentalities, methods, and capabilities to perpetrate violent crime. (see Situational Awareness and Self-Awareness.)

Criminal Justice - The study of criminal law and the procedures associated with its enforcement.

Criminology - The scientific study of crime and criminals.

Criss Cross - An entry maneuver which allows you to travel across a threshold quickly while employing a correct ready weapon position.

Cross Stepping - The process of crossing one foot in front or behind the other when moving.

Crushing Tactics - Nuclear grappling range techniques designed to crush the assailant's anatomical targets.

Cutting Accuracy - The ability to cut your assailant with precision and exactness.

Cutting Makeshift Weapon - One of the four types of CFA makeshift weapons. Any object or implement that can be used to effectively stab or slash an assailant. (see also Distracting Makeshift Weapon, Shielding Makeshift Weapon, and Striking Makeshift Weapon.)

Cylinder - The part of a revolver that holds cartridges in individual chambers.

D

Deadly Force - Weapons or techniques that may result in imminent, unconsciousness, permanent disfigurement, or death.

Deadly Weapon - An instrument designed to inflict serious bodily injury or death (e.g., firearms, impact tools, edged weapons).

Deception - A combative attribute. A stratagem whereby you delude your assailant.

Decisiveness - A combative attribute. The ability to follow a tactical course of action that is unwavering and focused.

De-escalation - One of the five possible tactical responses to a threatening situation. The science and art of diffusing a hostile individual without resorting to physical force. (see Assert, Comply, Escape and Fight Back).

De-escalation Stance - One of the many strategic stances used in the CFA system. A strategic and non aggressive stance used when diffusing a hostile individual.

Defense - The ability to strategically thwart an assailant's attack (armed or unarmed).

Defensive Flow - A progression of continuous defensive responses. Defensive Mentality - A defensive mind-set.

Defensive Range Manipulation (DRM) - The strategic manipulation of ranges (armed or unarmed) for defensive purposes.

Defensive Reaction Time - The elapsed time between an assailant's physical attack and your defensive response to that attack (see Offensive Reaction Time).

Demeanor - One of the essential factors to consider when assessing a threatening individual. A person's outward behavior.

Dependency - The dangerous phenomenon of solely relying on a particular person, agency, instrument, device, tool, animal, or weapon for self-defense and personal protection.

Destructions - A technique that strikes the assailant's attacking limb. Diet - A life-style of healthy eating.

Distance Gap - The spatial gap between the different ranges of armed and unarmed combat.

Distancing - The ability to quickly understand spatial relationships and how they relate to combat.

Distracting Makeshift Weapon - One of the four types of CFA makeshift weapons. An object that can be thrown into an assailant's face, body, or legs to distract him temporarily (see Cutting Makeshift Weapon, Striking Makeshift Weapon, and Shielding Makeshift Weapon.)

Distraction Tactics - Various verbal and physical tactics designed to distract your adversary.

Dojo - The Japanese term for "training hall."

Dominant Eye - The eye which is primarily used for aiming a firearm. The dominant eye is the one which is stronger and does more work.

Double-Action - A type of pistol action in which squeezing the trigger will both cock and release the hammer.

Drake Shooting - Shooting into places of likely cover.

Dry Firing - The process of shooting an unloaded firearm.

Duck - A defensive technique that permits you to evade your assailant's strike. Ducking is performed by dropping your body down and forward to avoid the assailant's blow.

E

Ectomorph - A body type classified by a high degree of slenderness, angularity, and fragility (see Endomorph and Mesomorph).

Effectiveness - One of the three criteria for a CFA body weapon, technique, tactic or maneuver. It means the ability to produce a desired effect (see Efficiency and Safety).

Efficiency - One of the three criteria for a CFA body weapon, technique, tactic or maneuver. It means the ability to reach an objective quickly and economically (see Effectiveness and Safety).

Ejector - The part of a pistol which ejects empty cartridge cases.

Embracing the Range - A ground fighting tactic whereby you pull or embrace your assailant.

Emotional Control - One of the nonverbal principles of strategic de-escalation. The ability to remain calm when faced with a hostile or threatening person.

Emotionless - A combative attribute. Being temporarily devoid of human feeling.

Endomorph - A body type classified by a high degree of roundness, softness, and body fat (see Ectomorph and Mesomorph).

Entry Method - A method that permits you to safely enter a combat range. Entry Technique - A technique that permits you to safely enter a combat range.

Entry Tool - A tool that permits you to safely enter a combat range.

Escape - Also known as tactical retreat. One of the five possible tactical responses to a threatening situation. To flee rapidly from the threat or danger. (See Comply, De-Escalate, Assert and Fight Back).

Escape Routes - Various avenues or exits that permit you to escape from a threatening individual or situation.

Evasion - A defensive maneuver that allows you to strategically maneuver your body away from the assailant's strike.

Evasive Sidestepping - Evasive footwork where the practitioner moves to either the right or left side.

Evasiveness - A combative attribute. The ability of avoid threat or danger. Evolution - A gradual process of change.

Excessive Force - An amount of force that exceeds the need for a particular event and is unjustified in the eyes of the law.

Experimentation - The painstaking process of testing a combative hypothesis or theory.

Explosiveness - A combative attribute that is characterized by a sudden outburst of violent energy.

F

Fake - Body movements that disguise your attack. This includes movements of the eyes, head, shoulders, knees, feet and in some cases the voice.

Fatal Funnel - A danger area that is created by openings such as doorways, windows, hallways, stairwells, etc.

Feed - (See Attachment.)

Fear - A strong and unpleasant emotion caused by the anticipation or awareness of threat or danger. There are three stages of fear in order of intensity: Fright, Panic, and Terror. (see Fright, Panic, Terror).

Feeler - A tool that tests the assailant's reaction time and overall abilities.

Feint - A tool that draws an offensive reaction from the assailant, thereby opening him up for a real strike. Feints are different from fakes because they are performed through the movement of an actual limb.

Femoral Nerve - A pressure point area located approximately six inches above the knee on the inside of the thigh.

Fight Back - One of the five possible tactical responses to a threatening situation. To use various physical and psychological tactics to either incapacitate or terminate a criminal assailant. (See Comply, Escape, Assert and De-Escalate.)

Fighting Stance - One of the different types of stances used in CFA's system. A strategic posture you can assume when face-to-face with an unarmed assailant (s). (See De-escalation Stance, Knife Defense Stance, Knife Fighting Stance, Firearms Stance, Natural Stance, Stick Fighting Stance).

Fight-or-Flight Syndrome - A response of the sympathetic nervous system to a fearful and threatening situation, during which it prepares your body to either fight or flee from the perceived danger.

Finesse - A combative attribute. The ability to skillfully execute a movement or a series of movements with grace and refinement.

Firearm Follow Through - Continuing to employ the shooting fundaments throughout the delivery of your shot.

First Strike Principle (FSP) - A CFA principle which states that when physical danger is imminent and you have no other tactical option but to fight back, you should strike first, strike fast, and strike with authority.

Flexibility - The muscles' ability to move through maximum natural ranges (see Muscular/Skeletal Conditioning).

Follow - A defensive technique used in the mid to long range of knife combat.

Forms - Traditional martial arts training methodology whereby the practitioner performs a series of prearranged movements that are based upon a response to imaginary opponents (see Kata).

Formlessness - A principle that rejects the essence of structure or system.

Footwork - Quick, economical steps performed on the balls of the feet while you are relaxed, alert, and balanced. Footwork is structured around four general movements: forward, backward, right, and left.

Fractal Cognizance -Being knowledgeable and aware of the fractal ranges and tools of combat.

Fright - The first stage of fear; quick and sudden fear (see Panic and Terror).

G

Gi - A traditional martial art uniform constructed of heavy cotton canvas material. The gi is commonly worn by practitioners of karate, judo, aikido, and jujitsu.

Grappling Range - One of the three ranges of unarmed combat. Grappling range is the closest distance of unarmed combat from which you can employ a wide variety of close-quarter tools and techniques. The grappling range of unarmed combat is also divided into two different planes: vertical (standing) and horizontal (ground fighting). (see Kicking Range and Punching Range)

Grappling Range Tools - The various body tools and

techniques that are employed in the grappling range of unarmed combat, including head butts; biting, tearing, clawing, crushing, and gouging tactics; foot stomps, horizontal, vertical, and diagonal elbow strikes, vertical and diagonal knee strikes, chokes, strangles, joint locks, and holds. (see and Kicking Range Tools).

Grapevine - A stabilizing technique used during a ground fight. The grapevine can be applied when you have either one (single leg grapevine) or both (double leg grapevine) of your feet hooked around the assailant's legs.

Ground Fighting - Fighting that takes place on the ground. (Also known as horizontal grappling plane).

Guard - 1) A fighter's hand positioning. 2) One of the positions used in ground fighting. The guard is a scissors hold applied with the legs.

H

Hammer - The moving part of a gun causes the firing pin to strike the cartridge primer.

Hammer Grip - A hand grip used to hold an edged weapon, bludgeon and some makeshift weapons; assumed when the top of the bludgeon or the tip of the edged weapon is pointing upwards.

Handgun - A firearm that can be held and discharged with one hand. Hand Positioning - (See Guard.)

Hang fire - A perceptible delay in the ignition of a cartridge after the primer has been struck.

Head-Hunter - A fighter who primarily attacks the head.

High-Line Kick - One of the two different classifications of a kick. A kick that is directed to targets above an assailant's waist level. (See Low-Line Kick.)

Histrionics - The field of theatrics or acting.

Homicide - The death of another person without legal justification of excuse.

Hook Kick - A circular kick that can be delivered in both kicking and punching ranges.

Hook Punch - A circular punch that can be delivered in both the punching and grappling ranges.

Hold - A specific manner of grasping or holding an assailant.

Human Shield - Using your assailant's body as a shield or obstacle in combat.

I

Ice Pick Grip - A hand grip used to hold an edged weapon, bludgeon and some makeshift weapons; assumed when the tip of the edged weapon or the top of the bludgeon is pointing downward.

Ice Pick Stick Strangle - A stick strangle used with an ice pick grip.

Immobilization Attack - One of the five conventional methods of attack. A highly complex system of moves and countermoves that allows you to temporarily control and manipulate the assailant's limbs (usually his arms and hands) in order to create an opening of attack.

Impact Power - Destructive force generated by mass and velocity.

Impact Training - A training exercise that develops pain tolerance.

Incapacitate - To disable an assailant by rendering him unconscious or damaging his bones, joints or organs.

Indirect Attack - One of the five conventional methods of attack. A progressive method of attack whereby the initial tool or technique is designed to set the assailant up for follow-up blows.

Initiation Phase - One of the three stages of a stick or bludgeon strike. The initiation phase is initiation point of a swing.

Insertion Points - Specific anatomical targets you can stab with a knife and some makeshift weapons.

Inside Position - The area between both of your assailant's arms where he has the greatest amount of control.

Intent - One of the essential factors to consider when assessing a threatening individual. The assailant's purpose or motive (see Demeanor, Positioning, Range, and Weapon Capability).

Intuition - The innate ability to know or sense something without the use of rational thought.

Intuitive Tool Response (ITR) - Spontaneously reacting with the appropriate combative tool.

J

Jab - A quick, probing punch designed to create openings in the assailant's defense.

Jeet Kune Do - "Way of Intercepting Fist." Bruce Lee's approach to the martial arts, which includes his innovative concepts, theories, methodologies, and philosophies of unarmed combat.

Joint Lock - A grappling range technique that immobilizes the assailant's joint.

Judo - "Gentle Way." A Japanese grappling art (founded by Jigoro Kano in 1882) which is used as a sport. Judo utilizes shoulder and hip throws, foot sweeps, chokes, and pins.

Jujitsu - "Gentleness" or "suppleness." A system of self-defense that is the parent of both Judo and Aikido. Jujitsu specializes in grappling range but is known to employ a few striking techniques.

K

Karate - "Empty hand" or "China hand," a traditional martial art that originated in Okinawa and later spread to Japan and Korea (see Kung-Fu).

Kata - "Pattern" or "Form". A traditional training methodology whereby the practitioner practices a series of prearranged movements.

Kick - 1) A sudden, forceful strike with the foot (see High-Line Kick and Low- Line Kick); 2) The recoil of a firearm.

Kick boxing - A popular combat sport that employs full-contact tools.

Kicking Range - One of the three ranges of unarmed combat. Kicking range is the furthest distance of unarmed combat wherein you use your legs to strike an assailant. (see Grappling Range and Punching Range).

Kicking Range Tools - The various body weapons employed in the kicking range of unarmed combat, including side kicks, push kicks, hook kicks, and vertical kicks.

Killer Instinct - A cold, primal mentality that surges to your consciousness and turns you into a vicious fighter.

Kinesics - The study of nonlinguistic body movement communications (i.e., eye movement, shrugs, facial gestures, etc.).

Kinesiology - The study of principles and mechanics of human movement.

Kinesthetic Perception - The ability to accurately feel your body during the execution of a particular movement.

Kneeling Firearm Stance - A strategic stance you assume when kneeling down with a handgun.

Knife-Defense Stance - One of the many stances used in

CFA's system. A strategic stance you assume when face-to-face with an knife or edged weapon attacker. (See De-escalation Stance, Fighting Stance, Knife Fighting Stance, Firearms Stance, Natural Stance, Stick Fighting Stance).

Kung-Fu - "Accomplished task or effort," a term used erroneously to identify the traditional Chinese martial arts (see Karate).

L

Lead Side -The side of the body that faces an assailant.

Leg Block - A blocking technique used with the legs. The leg block can be angled in three different directions: forward, right and left.

Limited Penetration - The (LP) is a corner clearing movement performed by positioning your firearm and one eye around the corner.

Linear Movement - Movements that follow the path of a straight line.

Long Range Combat - The furthest distance of knife and bludgeon combat. At this distance you can only strike or slash your assailant's hand.

Low Maintenance Tool - Offensive and defensive tools that require the least amount of training and practice to maintain proficiency. Low maintenance tools generally don't require preliminary stretching.

Low-Line Kick - One of the two different classifications of a kick. A kick that is directed to targets below the assailant's waist level. (See High-Line Kick.)

Lock - (see Joint Lock).

Loyalty - The state of being faithful to a person, cause, or ideal.

M

Makeshift Weapon - A common everyday object that can be converted into either an offensive or defensive weapon. There are four Makeshift Weapon classifications in the CFA system: Cutting Makeshift Weapons, Shielding Makeshift Weapons, Distracting Makeshift Weapons, and Striking Makeshift Weapons.

Maneuver - To manipulate into a strategically desired position.

Manipulation Accuracy - The ability to manipulate your assailant's limbs and joints with precision and exactness.

Martial Artist - One who studies and practices the martial arts.

Martial Arts - The traditional "arts of war" (see Karate and Kung-Fu).

Martial Truth - (See Combative Truth.)

Mechanics - (See Body Mechanics.)

Medicine Ball - A large, heavy ball used to strengthen and condition a fighter's stomach muscles.

Meet - A defensive technique that intercepts your assailant's line of attack with a slash.

Mental Attributes - The various cognitive qualities that enhance your fighting skills.

Mental Component - One of the three vital components of the CFA system. The mental component includes the cerebral aspects of fighting including the Killer Instinct, Strategic & Tactical Development, Analysis & Integration, Philosophy and Cognitive Development (see Physical Component and Spiritual Component).

Mesomorph - A body type classified by a high degree of muscularity and strength. (see Endomorph and Ectomorph).

Methods of Attack - The five conventionally recognized methods of attacking. They include: single attack, indirect attack, attack by draw, immobilization attack, and compound attack.

Mexican Standoff - A precarious situation where both you and your adversary have the drop on one another.

Mid Phase - One of the three stages of a stick swing. The mid phase is the contact or impact point of the swing.

Mid Range Combat - One of the three ranges of knife and bludgeon combat. At this distance you can strike, slash or stab your assailant's head, arms and body with your weapon.

Misfire - A failure of a cartridge to fire after the primer has been struck.

Mobility - A combative attribute. The ability to move your body quickly and freely while balanced. (see Footwork).

Modern Martial Art - A pragmatic combat art that has evolved to meet the demands and characteristics of the present time.

Modernist - One who subscribes to the philosophy of the modern martial arts.

Modification - To make fundamental changes to serve a new end.

Mounted Position - One of the five general ground fighting positions. The mounted position is where the practitioner sits on top of his assailant's torso or chest.

Mouthpiece - A rubber protector used to cover your teeth when sparring. There are two types of mouthpiece: single and double.

Muscular Endurance - The muscles' ability to perform the same motion or task repeatedly for a prolonged period of time.

Muscular Flexibility - The muscles' ability to move through maximum natural ranges.

Muscular Strength - The maximum force that can be exerted by a particular muscle or muscle group against resistance.

Muscular/Skeletal Conditioning - An element of physical fitness that entails muscular strength, endurance, and flexibility.

Muzzle - The front end of the barrel.

Muzzle Flash - An incandescent burst of light which is emitted from the muzzle and cylinder of a handgun.

N

Natural Stance - One of the many stances used in CFA's system. A strategic stance you assume when approached by a suspicious person who appears non threatening. (See De-escalation Stance, Fighting Stance, Knife Fighting Stance, Firearms Stance, Knife-Defense Stance, and Stick Fighting Stance).

Neutralize - (See Incapacitate.)

Neutral Zone - The distance outside of the kicking range from which neither the practitioner nor the assailant can touch the other.

Nomenclature Awareness - The ability to understand and recognize the system of names used in combat.

Non aggressive Physiology - Strategic body language used to de-escalate a potentially violent individual.

Non telegraphic Movement - Body mechanics or movements that do not inform an assailant of your intentions.

Nuclear Ground Fighting Tools - Specific grappling range tools designed to inflict immediate and irreversible damage. Some nuclear tools and tactics include: (1) Biting tactics; (2) Tearing tactics; (3) Crushing tactics; (4) Continuous Choking tactics; (5) Gouging techniques; (6) Raking tactics; (7) And all striking techniques.

O

OC (Oleoresin Capsicum, also known as pepper gas) -

A natural mixture of oil and cayenne pepper used as a self-defense spray. OC is an inflammatory agent that affects the assailant's mucus membranes (i.e. eyes, nose, throat, lungs).

Offense - The armed and unarmed means and methods of attacking a criminal assailant.

Offensive Flow - A progression of continuous offensive movements or actions designed to neutralize or terminate your adversary. (see Compound Attack).

Offensive Range Manipulation (ORM) - The strategic manipulation of ranges (armed or unarmed) for offensive purposes.

Offensive Reaction Time (ORT) - The elapsed time between target selection and target impaction.

One-Hand Reloading - The process of reloading a firearm with only one hand.

One-Mindedness - A state of deep concentration wherein you are free from all distractions (internal and external).

Opposite Poles - One of the ground fighting positions. The opposite pole position is assumed when both you and your assailant are facing opposite directions. This often occurs when sprawling against your adversary.

Ornamental Techniques - Techniques that are characterized as complex, inefficient, and or impractical for real combat situations.

P

Pain Tolerance - Your ability to physically and psychologically withstand pain. 490

Palming - The strategic concealment of a knife or edged weapon behind the forearm. Also known as Knife Palming.

Panic - The second stage of fear; overpowering fear (see Fright and Terror).

Parry - A defensive technique; a quick, forceful slap that redirects an assailant's linear attack.

Pass - A defensive technique used in knife fighting.

Patience - A combative attribute. The ability to endure and tolerate difficulty.

Perception - Interpretation of vital information acquired from your senses when faced with a potentially threatening situation.

Perpendicular Mount - One of the five general ground fighting positions. The perpendicular mount is established when you are lying on top of your adversary and both of your legs are on one side of his body.

Philosophical Resolution - The act of analyzing and answering various questions concerning the use of violence in defense of yourself and others.

Philosophy - One of the five aspects of CFA's mental component. A deep state of introspection whereby you methodically resolve critical questions concerning the use of force in defense of yourself or others.

Physical Attributes - The numerous physical qualities that enhance your combative skills and abilities.

Physical Component - One of the three vital components of the CFA system. The physical component includes the physical aspects of fighting including Physical Fitness, Weapon/Technique Mastery, and Combative Attributes (see Mental Component and Spiritual Component).

Physical Conditioning - (See Combative Fitness).

Pistol - A gun with a short barrel that can be held, aimed, and fired with one hand.

Power - A physical attribute of armed and unarmed combat. The amount of force you can generate when striking an anatomical target.

Physical Fitness - (See Combative Fitness).

Pitch - One of the four components of the human voice. The relative highness or lowness of the voice.

Poker Face - A neutral and attentive facial expression that is used when de- escalating a hostile individual. The poker face prevents a hostile person from reading your intentions or feelings.

Positioning - The spatial relationship of the assailant to the assailed person in terms of target exposure, escape, angle of attack, and various other strategic considerations.

Positions of Concealment - Various objects or locations that permit you to temporarily hide from your adversary. Positions of Concealment are most commonly used to evade engagement with your assailant(s) and they permit you to attack with the element of surprise. Positions of Concealment include: trees, shrubbery, behind doors, the dark, walls, stairwells, under cars, large and tall objects, etc.

Positions of Cover - Any object or location that temporarily protects you from the assailant's gun fire. Some Positions of Cover include: large concrete utility poles, large rocks, thick trees, an engine block, corner of a building, concrete steps, etc.

Post Traumatic Syndrome (PTS) - A group of symptoms that may occur in the aftermath of a violent confrontation with a criminal assailant. Common symptoms of Post Traumatic Syndrome include denial, shock, fear, anger, severe depression, sleeping and eating disorders, societal withdrawal, and paranoia.

Power Generator - (See Anatomical Power Generators)

Premise - An axiom, concept, rule or any other valid reason to modify or go beyond that which has been established.

Pressure Point - a vulnerable anatomical target, such as nerve cluster, joint or any other sensitive tissue target that can be struck, compressed, or wrenched with force.

227

Probable Reaction Dynamics (PRD) - the opponent's anticipated or predicted movements or actions during both armed and unarmed combat.

Probe -A offensive tool that tests the assailant's combative abilities.

Proficiency Training - A CFA training methodology requiring the practitioner to execute a specific body weapon, technique, maneuver or tactic over and over for a prescribed number or repetitions (see Conditioning Training and Street Training).

Progressive Indirect Attack -(see Indirect Attack).

Proxemics - The study of the nature and effect of man's personal space.

Proximity - The ability to maintain a strategically safe distance from a threatening individual.

Pseudospeciation - A combative attribute. The tendency to assign subhuman and inferior qualities to a threatening assailant.

Psychological Conditioning - The process of conditioning the mind for the horrors and rigors of real combat.

Psycho/Emotional Training - Combative training conducted when you're experiencing different types of emotional states.

Psychomotor Domain - This includes the physical skills and attributes necessary to execute a combative tool, technique or maneuver.

Psychopath - A person with an antisocial personality disorder, especially one manifested in aggressive, perverted, criminal, or amoral behavior.

Pummel - A flurry of full-speed, full-force strikes delivered from the mounted position.

Punch - A quick, forceful strike of the fists.

Punching Range - One of the three ranges of unarmed combat. Punching range is the mid range of unarmed combat from which the fighter uses his hands to strike his assailant. (see Kicking Range and Grappling Range)

Punching Range Tools - The various body weapons that are employed in the punching range of unarmed combat, including finger jabs, palm heel strikes, rear cross, knife hand strikes, horizontal and shovel hooks, uppercuts, and hammer fist strikes. (see Grappling Range Tools and Kicking Range Tools).

Q

Qualities of Combat - (see Attributes of Combat).

Quick Peek - A technique which is executed from a position of cover by rapidly darting out a small portion of your head and one eye to quickly observe.

R

Range - The spatial relationship between a fighter and a threatening assailant.

Range Deficiency - The inability to effectively fight and defend in all ranges (armed and unarmed) of combat.

Range Manipulation - A combative attribute. The strategic manipulation of combat ranges.

Range Proficiency - A combative attribute. The ability to effectively fight and defend in all ranges (armed and unarmed) of combat.

Ranges of Armed Combat - The various distances a fighter might physically engage with an assailant while involved in armed combat: including knives, bludgeons, projectiles, make-shift weapons, and firearms.)

Ranges of Engagement - (See Combat Ranges).

Ranges of Unarmed Combat - The three distances a fighter might physically engage with an assailant while involved in unarmed combat: kicking range, punching range, and grappling range.

Reaction Dynamics - The assailant's physical response to a particular tool, technique, or weapon after initial contact is made.

Reaction Time - The elapsed time between a stimulus and the response to that particular stimulus (see Offensive Reaction Time and Defensive Reaction Time).

Rear Cross - A straight punch delivered from the rear hand that crosses from right to left (if in a left stance) or left to right (if in a right stance).

Rear Side - The side of the body furthest from the assailant (see Lead Side).

Reasonable Force - That degree of force which is not excessive for a particular event and which is appropriate in protecting yourself or others.

Refinement - The strategic and methodical process of improving or perfecting.

Repetition - Performing a single movement, exercise, strike or action continuously for a specific period.

Research - A scientific investigation or inquiry.

Rest Position - A relaxed posture you assume (when holding a stick or bludgeon) during idle periods in class (i.e., talking to another students, receiving instructions, etc.).

Reverberation Path - The path at which your stick or bludgeon can bounce back at you.

Revolver - A handgun consisting of a cylinder that brings several chambers successively into line with the barrel of the gun.

Rhythm - Movements characterized by the natural ebb and flow of related elements.

Right to Bear Arms - A provision of the Second Amendment to the United States Constitution that prohibits our government from interfering with the right of the people to arm themselves.

Rimfire - A firearm cartridge which has its primer located around the rim of the case bottom.

Round - 1) A period of time. 2) A single unit of ammunition (see Cartridge).

S

Safe Room - A strategic location in your residence where you and family members can escape from an intruder who has entered your home.

Safety - One of the three criteria for a CFA body weapon, technique, maneuver or tactic. It means the that the tool, technique, maneuver or tactic provides the least amount of danger and risk for the practitioner (see Efficiency and Effectiveness).

Scissors Hold - (see Guard).

Secondary Hand - A close quarter technique used in both knife and bludgeon fighting whereby you temporarily hold your assailant's weapon hand in place after you have employed a defensive maneuver.

Secondary Weapons - Various natural body weapons that are applied during armed combat.

Selective Semantics - The selection and utilization of strategic words to de-escalate a hostile person. Also known as Choice Words.

Self-Awareness - One of the three categories of CFA awareness. Knowing and understanding yourself. This includes aspects of yourself which may provoke criminal violence and which will promote a proper and strong reaction to an attack. (see Criminal Awareness and Situational

Awareness.)

Self-Confidence - Having trust and faith in yourself.

Self-Defense - The act of defending yourself or one's family (also called Personal Protection or Self-Protection).

Self-Enlightenment - The state of knowing your capabilities, limitations, character traits, feelings, general attributes, and motivations (see Self- Awareness.)

Semiautomatic Handgun - (see Autoloader).

Sensei - Teacher.

Set - A term used to describe a grouping of repetitions.

Setup Tool - A tool used to throw the assailant off balance and/or open his defenses.

Shadow Fighting - A CFA training exercise used to develop and refine your tools, techniques, and attributes of armed and unarmed combat.

Shielding Makeshift Weapon - One of the four types of CFA makeshift weapons. Any object that can be used to effectively shield oneself from an assailant's attack (see also Distracting Makeshift Weapon, Cutting Makeshift Weapon, and Striking Makeshift Weapon.)

Shooting Accuracy - The ability to shoot a firearm with precision and exactness.

Shot - A package or wad of metal balls that vary in size and spread out as they travel away from the muzzle of a shot gun.

Shotgun - A single-or double-barreled, smooth-bore firearm used for firing shot or slugs at a relatively close distance.

Shoulder Roll - A defensive technique that rocks your body away from a punch in order to nullify its force.

Side Fall - A firearm engagement technique which is executed from a kneeling position behind cover.

Sifu - (See Sensei.)

Sight Alignment - A component of marksmanship whereby you correctly align your dominant eye with both the front and rear sights of your firearm.

Sights - Various electronic, optical, and mechanical devices used to aim a firearm.

Single Action - A type of pistol action in which pulling the trigger will release the hammer.

Single Attack - One of the five conventional methods of attack. A method of attack whereby you deliver a solitary offensive strike. It may involve a series of discreet probes or one swift, powerful strike aimed at terminating the encounter. (See Compound Attack, Indirect Attack, Immobilization Attack, and Attack By Draw).

Situational Awareness - One of the three categories of CFA awareness. A state of being totally alert to your immediate surroundings, including people, places, objects, and actions. (see Criminal Awareness and Self-Awareness.)

Skeletal Alignment - The proper alignment or arrangement of your body. Skeletal Alignment maximizes the structural integrity of striking tools.

Slash - One of the two ways to cut someone with a knife or edged weapon. A quick, sweeping stroke of a knife (see Stab.)

Slipping - A defensive maneuver that permits you to avoid an assailant's linear blow without stepping out of range. Slipping can be accomplished by quickly snapping the head and upper torso sideways (right or left) to avoid the blow.

Snap Back - A defensive maneuver that permits you to avoid an assailant's linear and circular blow without stepping out of range. The snap back can be accomplished by quickly snapping the head backwards to avoid the assailant's blow.

Somatotyping - A method of classifying human body types or builds into three different categories: ectomorph, mesomorph, and endomorph.

Speed - A physical attribute of armed and unarmed combat. The rate or a measure of the rapid rate of motion.

Spinning Kicks - Kicks delivered with a spin of the body.

Spinning Punches - Punches delivered with a spin of the body.

Spiritual Component - One of the three vital components of the CFA system. The spiritual component includes the metaphysical issues and aspects of existence (see Physical Component and Mental Component).

Sprawling - A defensive technique in grappling range. The sprawl technique is accomplished by lowering your hips to the ground while simultaneously shooting both of your legs back.

Square-Off - To be face-to-face with a hostile or threatening assailant who is about to attack you.

Squib Load - A cartridge which develops less than normal velocity after the ignition of a cartridge.

Stab - One of the two ways to cut someone with a knife or edged weapon. A quick thrust made with a pointed weapon or implement, usually a knife. (see Slash.)

Stable Terrain - Terrain which is principally characterized as stationary, compact, dense, hard, flat, dry, or solid.

Stance - One of the many strategic postures that you assume prior to or during armed or unarmed combat.

Stance Selection - A combative attribute. The ability to instinctively select a stance appropriate for a particular combat situation.

Standing Firearm Stance - A strategic stance you assume when standing with a handgun.

Step and Drag - Strategic footwork used when standing on unstable terrain. Stick Block - A defensive technique that stops your assailant's stick strike.

Stick Deflection - A defensive technique that deflects and redirects your assailant's stick strike.

Stick Twirl - A dexterity exercise performed with either one or two sticks. Stop-Hit - A method of hitting the assailant before his tool reaches full extension.

Stopping Power - A firearm's ability to stop the assailant from continuing any further action.

Strategic Leaning - A defensive maneuver which permits you to evade a knife slash while remaining in range to counter.

Strategic Positioning - Tactically positioning yourself to either escape, move behind a barrier, or use a makeshift weapon.

Strategy - A carefully planned method of achieving your goal of engaging an assailant under advantageous conditions.

Street Fight - A spontaneous and violent confrontation between two or more individuals wherein no rules apply.

Street Fighter - An unorthodox combatant who has no formal training. His combative skills and tactics are usually developed in the street by the process of trial and error.

Street Smarts - Having the knowledge, skills and attitude necessary to avoid, defuse, confront, and neutralize both armed and unarmed assailants.

Street Training - A CFA training methodology requiring the practitioner to deliver explosive compound attacks for ten to twenty seconds (see Conditioning Training and Proficiency Training).

Strength Training - The process of developing muscular strength through systematic application of progressive resistance.

Striking Accuracy - The ability to strike your assailant with precision and exactness (this includes natural body weapons, bludgeons and some makeshift weapons).

Striking Art - A combat art that relies predominantly on

235

striking techniques to neutralize or terminate a criminal attacker.

Striking Tool - 1) A natural body weapon that impacts with the assailant's anatomical target. 2) A hand-held implement that impacts with the assailant's anatomical target.

Striking Makeshift Weapon - One of the four types of CFA makeshift weapons. Any object that can be used to effectively strike a criminal assailant (see also Distracting Makeshift Weapon, Cutting Makeshift Weapon, and Shielding Makeshift Weapon.)

Strong Side - The strongest and most coordinated side of your body. Structure - A definite and organized pattern.

Style - The distinct manner in which a fighter executes or performs his combat skills.

Stylistic Integration - The purposeful and scientific collection of tools and techniques from various disciplines, which are strategically integrated and dramatically altered to meet three essential criteria: efficiency, effectiveness, and combative safety.

System - The unification of principles, philosophies, rules, strategies, methodologies, tools, and techniques or a particular method of combat.

T

Tactical Calming - (See De-Escalation.)

Tactic - The skill of using the available means to achieve an end.

Tactical Option Selection - A combative attribute. The ability to select the appropriate tactical option for any particular self-defense situation.

Tactile Sight - A combative attribute. The ability to "see" through tactile contact with your assailant.

Takedowns -Various grappling maneuvers designed to take your assailant down to the ground.

Target Exploitation - A combative attribute. The strategic maximization of your assailant's reaction dynamics during a fight. Target Exploitation can be applied in both armed and unarmed encounters.

Target Impaction - The successful striking of the appropriate anatomical target.

Target Orientation - A combative attribute. Having a workable knowledge of the assailant's anatomical targets. Target orientation is divided into five different categories: (1) Impact Targets - anatomical targets that can be struck with your natural body weapons; (2) Non-Impact Targets - anatomical targets that can be strangled, twisted, torn, crushed, clawed, gouged, broken, dislocated, or strategically manipulated; (3) Edged Weapon Targets - anatomical targets that can be punctured or slashed with a knife or edged weapon; (4) Bludgeon Targets - anatomical targets that can be struck with a stick or bludgeon; (5) Ballistic Targets - anatomical targets that can be shot by a firearm.

Target Recognition - The ability to immediately recognize appropriate anatomical targets during an emergency self-defense situation.

Target Selection - The process of mentally selecting the appropriate anatomical target for your self-defense situation. This is predicated on certain factors, including proper force response, assailant's positioning and range.

Target Stare - A form of telegraphing whereby you stare at the anatomical target you intend to strike.

Target Zones - The three areas which an assailant's anatomical targets are located. (See Zone One, Zone Two and Zone Three.)

Technique - A systematic procedure by which a task is accomplished.

Telegraphic Cognizance - A combative attribute. The ability to recognize both verbal and non-verbal signs of aggression or assault.

Telegraphing - Unintentionally making your intentions known to your adversary. Tempo - The speed or rate at which you speak.

Terrain - The type of surface that you are standing on. There are two classifications of terrain: stable and unstable. (See Stable Terrain and Unstable Terrain)

Terrain Orientation - A combative attribute. Having a working knowledge of the various types of environmental terrains and their advantages, dangers, and strategic limitations.

Terror - The third stage of fear; defined as overpowering fear (see Fright and Panic).

Throw - Grappling techniques designed to unbalance your assailant and lift him off the floor.

Timing - A physical and mental attribute or armed and unarmed combat. Your ability to execute a movement at the optimum moment.

Tone - The overall quality or character of your voice.

Tool - (See Body Weapon.)

Traditional Style/System - (See Traditional Martial Art.)

Traditionalism - The beliefs and principles of a traditional or classical martial art.

Traditionalist - One who subscribes to the principles and practices of traditional martial arts.

Traditional Martial Arts - Any martial art that fails to evolve and meet the demands and characteristics of the present time (see Karate and Kung-Fu).

Training Drills - The various exercises and drills aimed at perfecting combat skills, attributes, and tactics.

Training Methodologies - Training procedures utilized in the CFA system.

Training Zone - The training zone (or target heart rate) is a safe and effective level of physical activity that produces cardiorespiratory fitness.

Trapping - Momentarily immobilizing or manipulating the assailant's limb or limbs in order to create an opening to attack.

Trapping Range - The distance between punching and grappling range in which trapping techniques are attempted.

Traversing Skills - Pivoting and twisting laterally. Traversing skills can be used for both armed and unarmed combat.

Trigger Squeeze - A component of marksmanship. Trigger Squeeze is achieved by squeezing the trigger of your firearm straight to the rear in a smooth and fluid manner without disturbing the sight alignment.

Trouble Shooting Skills - A combative attribute. The ability to immediately diagnose and solve problems when engaged with the adversary.

U

Unified Mind - A mind which is free and clear of distractions and focused on the combative situation.

Uniform Crime Report (UCR) - A nationwide cooperative statistical compilation of the efforts and reports of 16,000 state and local law enforcement agencies that voluntarily report data on crime.

Unstable Terrain - Terrain which is characterized as mobile, uneven, flexible, slippery, wet, or rocky. (See Stable Terrain).

Unstructured Modernist - A martial artist who adheres to the abstract principles of combative formlessness.

Use of Force Response - A combative attribute. Selecting the appropriate level of force for a particular emergency self-defense situation.

V

V-Grip - A strategically defensive grip used to defend against an edged weapon attack.

Vertical Trapping - Trapping techniques that are applied while standing face to face with your adversary. (See Immobilization Attack).

Viciousness - A combative attribute. Dangerously aggressive behavior. Victim - Any person who is the object of a particular crime.

Visualization - The purposeful formation of mental images and scenarios in the mind's eye.

Visual Monitoring Points - Specific points or locations on your assailant that you should look at during an emergency self-defense situation.

W

Warm-up - A series of mild exercises, stretches, and movement designed to prepare you for more intense exercise.

Weak Side - The weakest and most uncoordinated side of your body.

Weapon and Technique Mastery - A component of CFA's physical component. The kinesthetic and psychomotor development of a weapon or combative technique.

Weapon Capability - An assailant's ability to use and attack with a particular weapon.

Weapon Hierarchy Mastery - Possessing the knowledge, skills and attitude necessary to master the complete hierarchy of combat weapons.

Weapon Uniformity - Gripping and/or drawing your hand-held weapon the same way every time.

Webbing - The first phase of the Widow Maker Program. Webbing is a two hand strike delivered to the assailant's chin.

It is called Webbing because your hands resemble a large web that wraps around the enemy's face.

Western Boxing - A Western combat sport that only employs punching-range tools.

Widow Maker Program – A CFA program specifically designed to teach the law abiding citizen how to use extreme force when faced with immediate threat of unlawful deadly criminal attack. The Widow Maker program is divided into two phases or methodologies: Webbing and Razing.

Y

Yell - A loud and aggressive scream or shout used for various strategic reasons.

Z

Zero Beat – One of the four beat classifications of the Widow Maker, Feral Fighting and Savage Street Fighting Programs. Zero beat strikes are full pressure techniques applied to a specific target until ruptures. They include gouging, crushing, biting, and choking techniques.

Zone One - Anatomical targets related to your senses, including the eyes, temple, nose, chin, and back of neck.

Zone Three - Anatomical targets related to your mobility, including thighs, knees, shins, and instep.

Zone Two - Anatomical targets related to your breathing, including front of neck, solar plexus, ribs, and groin.

Zoning - A defensive maneuver designed to negate your assailant's stick strike through strategic movement and precise timing. Zoning can be accomplished by either moving into the direction of your assailant's strike (before it generates significant force) or by moving completely out of his stick's arc.

Suggested Reading & Viewing

SUGGESTED READING (BOOKS):

• Engage With Rage: A Real-World Guide to Close Quarter Self-Defense

• War Machine II: Real-World Self-Defense Combatives for Everyone

• Combat Pressure Points: A No Nonsense Guide To Pressure Point Fighting for Self-Defense

• Boxing Domination: A 21-Day Program to Psych-Out, Confuse, Frustrate, and Beat Your Opponent in Boxing and MMA

• Power Boxing Workout Secrets

• Speed Boxing Secrets: A 21-Day Program to Hitting Faster and Reacting Quicker in Boxing and Martial Arts

• Knife Fighting: A Step-by-Step Guide to Practical Knife Fighting for Self-Defense

• The 10 Best Knife Fighting Techniques

• The 10 Best Power Punches: For Boxing, Martial Arts, MMA and Self-Defense

• The 10 Best Mental Toughness Exercises

• The 10 Best Ways to Defeat Multiple Attackers

• The 10 Best Ways to Develop Your Killer Instinct:

• The 10 Best Bar Fighting Moves: Down and Dirty Fighting Techniques to Save Your Ass When Things Get Ugly

• The 10 Best Sucker Punch Tricks

• Survival Weapons: A User's Guide to the Best Self-Defense Weapons for Any Dangerous Situation

• Knockout: The Ultimate Guide to Sucker Punching

• The 10 Best Kicking Techniques

• The 10 Best Stick Fighting Techniques

• Cane Fighting: The Authoritative Guide to Using the Cane or Walking Stick for Self-Defense

• The Heavy Bag Bible: 3 Best-Selling Heavy Bag Books In One Massive Collection

• Double End Bag Workout

- The 10 Best Things To Do When Held At Gunpoint
- The 10 Best Ways To Defeat Multiple Attackers
- The 10 Best Things To Do During a Mass Shooting
- The 10 Best Stick Fighting Techniques
- Bruce Lee's 5 Methods of Attack
- The Widow Maker Compendium (Books 1-3)
- Heavy Bag Workout
- Heavy Bag Combinations
- Invincible: Mental Toughness Techniques for the Street, Battlefield and Playing Field
- Unleash Hell
- Feral Fighting
- Savage Street Fighting
- Stand and Deliver
- The Widow Maker Program
- Maximum Damage
- Kubotan Power
- The Complete Body Opponent Bag Book
- Self-Defense Tips & Tricks
- Heavy Bag Training: Boxing, Mixed Martial Arts & Self-Defense
- Out of the Cage: A Complete Guide to Beating a Mixed Martial Artist on the Street
- Gun Safety: For Home Defense and Concealed Carry
- Warrior Wisdom: Inspiring Ideas from the World's Greatest Warriors
- Ground War: How to Destroy a Grappler in a Street Fight
- 1001 Street Fighting Secrets: The Principles of Contemporary Fighting Arts
- War Machine: How to Transform Yourself into a Vicious and Deadly Street Fighter
- The Bigger They Are, The Harder They Fall: How to Defeat a Larger & Stronger Adversary in a Street Fight
- First Strike: Mastering the Preemptive Strike for Street Combat

• When Seconds Count: Everyone Guide to Self Defense

• Killer Instinct: Unarmed Combat for Street Survival

• Street Lethal: Unarmed Urban Combat

SUGGESTED VIEWING (VIDEOS):

• Pressure Point Fighting: The Science of Striking Vital Targets

• Combat Energy Drills

• Punching Mitts: Drills & Workout Routines

• Judge, Jury & Executioner

• Pepper Spray: A Video Guide to Using Pepper Spray for Self Defense

• Sparring: Tips: Tips, Tactics & Techniques to Dominate Your Opponent

• Kubotans & Yawaras: A Quick & Dirty Guide

• Submission Fighting for the Street (Volume 1)

• Submission Fighting for the Street (Volume 2)

• Submission Fighting for the Street (Volume 3)

• Medicine Ball Workout (Volume 1)

• Medicine Ball Workout (Volume 2)

• Double End Bag Training

• Heavy Bag Training

• Power Punching

• Speed Training for Street Fighting (Volume 1): Visual Reflexes

• Speed Training for Street Fighting (Volume 2): Tactile Reflexes

• Speed Training for Street Fighting (Volume 3): Recognition & Auditory Reflexes

• Speed Training for Street Fighting (Volume 4): Movement Speed

• Wrist Locks For The Street (Volume 1)

• Wrist Locks For The Street (Volume 2)

• Choke Out

• Body Opponent Bag Training

PUNISHING PRESSURE POINTS

• War Machine II

• Sneak Peek

• Armed to the Teeth (Volume 1)

• Armed to the Teeth (Volume 2)

• Defend or Die

• Escape Master

• In Your Face

• Engage With Rage

• First Strike

• Ground Fighting in The Streets

• Batter Up

• Under The Gun

• Street Stick Fighting

• Use It or Lose It

• Rat Packed

•,Ground Pounders

• Control & Conquer (Volume 1)

• Control & Conquer (Volume 2)

• Savage Street Fighting: Tactical Savagery As A Last Resort

• The WidowMaker Program: Maximum Punishment for Extreme Situations

• Feral Fighting Program: Level 2 WidowMaker

• War Blade Program: A Complete Guide to Tactical Knife Fighting

About Sammy Franco

With over 35 years of experience, Sammy Franco is one of the world's foremost authorities on armed and unarmed self-defense. Highly regarded as a leading innovator in combat sciences, Mr. Franco was one of the premier pioneers in the field of "reality-based" self-defense and martial arts instruction.

Sammy Franco is perhaps best known as the founder and creator of Contemporary Fighting Arts (CFA), a state-of-the-art offensive- based combat system that is specifically designed for real-world self-defense.

CFA is a sophisticated and practical system of self-defense, designed specifically to provide efficient and effective methods to avoid, defuse, confront, and neutralize both armed and unarmed attackers.

Sammy Franco has frequently been featured in martial art magazines, newspapers, and appeared on numerous radio and television programs. Mr. Franco has also authored numerous books, magazine articles, and editorials, and has developed a massive library of instructional videos.

Sammy Franco's experience and credibility in the combat sciences is unequaled. One of his many accomplishments in this field includes the fact that he has earned the ranking of a Law Enforcement Master Instructor, and has designed, implemented, and taught officer survival training to the United States Border Patrol (USBP).

He has instructed members of the US Secret Service,

Military Special Forces, Washington DC Police Department, Montgomery County, Maryland Deputy Sheriffs, and the US Library of Congress Police. Sammy Franco is also a member of the prestigious International Law Enforcement Educators and Trainers Association (ILEETA) as well as the American Society of Law Enforcement Trainers (ASLET) and he is listed in the "Who's Who Director of Law Enforcement Instructors."

Sammy Franco is a nationally certified Law Enforcement Instructor in the following curricula: PR-24 Side-Handle Baton, Police Arrest and Control Procedures, Police Personal Weapons Tactics, Police Power Handcuffing Methods, Police Oleoresin Capsicum Aerosol Training (OCAT), Police Weapon Retention and Disarming Methods, Police Edged Weapon Countermeasures and "Use of Force" Assessment and Response Methods.

Mr. Franco holds a Bachelor of Arts degree in Criminal Justice from the University of Maryland. He is a regularly featured speaker at a number of professional conferences and conducts dynamic and enlightening seminars on numerous aspects of self-defense and combat training.

On a personal level, Sammy Franco is an animal lover, who will go to great lengths to assist and rescue animals. Throughout the years, he's rescued everything from turkey vultures to goats. However, his most treasured moments are always spent with his beloved German Shepherd dogs.

For more information about Mr. Franco and his unique system of self-defense, you can visit his website at: ContemporaryFightingArts.com

Made in the USA
Las Vegas, NV
11 November 2024

11589349R00144